Teachers

Emotional Intelligence and Teaching Effectiveness

Shazia Kanwal

Dedication

To

My late Baba Abdul Jabbar, my mother (Rukhsana Shaheen), and my daughters Munazza Batool and Izzah Fatima, who drives me through the valley of obscurity with the light of trust, encouragement and support.

ACRONYMS

B.Ed.	Bachelor of Education
BISE	Board of Intermediate and Secondary Education
CMS	Classroom Management Skills
CVI	Content Validity Index
CVR	Content Validity Ratio
EMIS	Educational Management Information System
EI	Emotional Intelligence
EIQ	Emotional Intelligence Questionnaire
EIS	Emotional Intelligence Scale
ESAS	Emotional Self-Awareness Scale
ESRS	Emotional Self-Regulation Scale
GTCS	General Teaching Competency Scale
HSC	Higher Secondary Certificate
ISS	Interpersonal Skills Scale
JS	Job Stress
M.Ed.	Masters of Education
M.Phil.	Masters of Philosophy
MA	Master in Arts
MSC	Master in Science
MBI- ES	Maslach Burnout Inventory-Educators Survey
MI	Multiple Intelligence
MIT	Multiple Intelligence Theory
MEIS	Multifactor Emotional Intelligence Scale

Ph.D.	Doctor of Philosophy
RMS	Relationship Management Skills
SRMEI	Self-Report Measure of Emotional Intelligence
STP	Student Teacher Performance
TES	Teacher Effectiveness Scale
TRS	Teacher Rating Scale
TSES	Teachers' Sense of Efficacy Scale
TPS	Teaching and Pedagogical Skills
TE	Teaching Effectiveness
Teique-SF	Trait Emotional Intelligence Questionnaire Short Form
UNESCO	United Nations Educational, Scientific and Cultural Organization

TABLE OF CONTENTS

LIST OF TABLES

LIST OF FIGURES

ABSTRACT

Emotional Intelligence (EI) is an important psychological construct and its thorough understanding is necessary for enhancing teachers' effectiveness. This important concept has failed to get the attention of researchers in Pakistan. Presently teacher preparation and recruitment policy focus on content expertise. There is no formal mechanism of assessment and development of Emotional Intelligence during teacher education or at the time of recruitment. The affective or emotional face of teaching is normally overlooked. The main purpose of the study was to analyze the relationship between teachers' Emotional Intelligence and its impact on teaching effectiveness at Higher Secondary level in Khyber Pakhtunkhwa. Find out the teachers' Emotional Self-Regulation Skills and their impact on teaching effectiveness at the higher secondary level in Khyber Pakhtunkhwa. Objectives of the study were to analyze teachers' Emotional Self-Awareness Skills, Emotional Self-Regulation Skills, Interpersonal Skills, overall Emotional Intelligence and their impact on teaching effectiveness at the higher secondary level in Khyber Pakhtunkhwa. The hypotheses of the study were that there is no significant relationship between teachers' Emotional Self-Regulation Skills and Teaching Effectiveness. There is no significant relationship between teachers' Emotional Self-Awareness Skills and Teaching Effectiveness. There is no significant relationship between teachers' Interpersonal Skills and Teaching Effectiveness. There is no significant relationship between teacher's demographic variables (gender, marital status, age and qualification) and EI. There is no significant relationship between EI of teachers and their Teaching Effectiveness.

At the first stage of sampling the researcher using cluster sampling technique selected seven districts of Khyber Pakhtunkhwa. At the second stage three hundred and fifty-seven (357) teachers were selected as sample of the study using Krejcie and Morgan sample table. At the third stage of sampling, a proportional number of higher secondary schools were selected to represent the whole population using stratified sampling. Two hundred and forty-three (243) male teachers from higher secondary schools for boys and one hundred and fourteen (114) female teachers from higher secondary schools for girls were selected at this stage. A total number of six (06) teachers and (30) Students were selected as the sample of the study from one school.

Data was collected using the instrument Self-Report Measure of Emotional Intelligence (SRMEI) and Teaching Effectiveness Scale (TES). Self-Report Measure of Emotional Intelligence was used to measure the Emotional Intelligence of teachers at the higher secondary level. SRMEI was adopted from the National Institute of Psychology Quaid-e-Azam University Islamabad. SRMEI is a 60 items Self-Report Instrument. The test comprises three sub-scales i.e. (a) Emotional Self-Regulation Scale (b) Emotional Self-Awareness Scale, (c) Interpersonal Skills Scale. To measure Teachers' Effectiveness researcher developed the Teaching Effectiveness Scale (TES). Content validity of the TES was established through the judgement of subject and field experts. The reliability coefficient of the final instrument was 0.87. The final version of Teaching Effectiveness Scale comprised three sub factors i.e. (a) Teaching and Pedagogical Skills (TPS), (b) Classroom Management Skills (CMS) and Relationship Management Skills (RMS). The pilot study included 50 students and it aimed to enhance the reliability and validity of the study.

SPSS version-20 software was used to analyze the data. The mean score of respondents on SRMEI and TES were calculated with SPSS. Independent Sample T-test, ANOVA and Pearson Correlation were applied for analysis.

The results of the study discovered that there was a positive relationship between teachers' Emotional Intelligence and their Teaching Effectiveness at higher secondary schools in Khyber Pakhtunkhwa. They indicated a low level of teachers' socio-emotional intelligence with room for improvement. The researcher found a significant relationship between all the variables of Emotional Intelligence and Teaching Effectiveness i.e. Emotional Self-Management, Emotional Self-Awareness, Interpersonal Skills and Teaching and pedagogical Skills, Classroom Management Skills and Relationship Management Skills. Female teachers were found significantly better than their male counterparts on all the sub-scales of SRMEI i.e. (a) Emotional Self-Management (b) Emotional Self-Awareness and (c) Interpersonal Skills. Married teachers also scored slightly higher than single teachers on all the sub scales and overall EI. All four age groups were neither significantly different from one another on any of the sub scales nor overall EI. Teachers' qualifications were also found to be significantly linked with enhanced EI skills. Finally all the facets of teachers' Emotional Intelligence i.e. Emotional Self-Awareness, Emotional Self-Regulation Skills, Interpersonal Skills and overall SRMEI were positively correlated with all the facets of Teaching Effectiveness i.e. Teaching and Pedagogical Skills, Classroom Management Skills, Relationship Management Skills and overall Teaching Effectiveness.

This study has provided effective information about the influence and impact of teachers' Emotional intelligence on their teaching effectiveness. In Pakistan still, IQ is considered as the only true reflector of a person's capabilities and given importance in teachers' selection and training mechanism. Findings may guide improvement in teachers' selection and promotions criteria. It can contribute to shifting the concern of authorities to valuing Emotional Intelligence along with Cognitive Intelligence as a prerequisite for effective teaching. The study provides evidence for the incorporation of Emotional Intelligence skills in pre-service and in-service teacher training programs. This study helps improve in teacher evaluation system which currently assesses only content-related issues and entirely ignore the emotional component of teaching. It may also bring an impetus for future experimental studies regarding the effects of Emotional Intelligence intervention on Teaching Effectiveness.

CHAPTER-I

INTRODUCTION

1.1   Rationale of the study

After the dominance of cognitive intelligence in the 20th century, it is now an interesting phenomenon that highlights that success only in academia or professional life isn't simply the result of virtuous IQ-scores (McClelland, 1973; Goleman, 1995). This fact leads to the promotion of an advanced concept in the field of intelligence i.e. Emotional Intelligence (EI).The origins of the basic idea of EI can be traced back to Thorndike's earlier idea of Social Intelligence. Thorndike describes Social Intelligence as an individual's ability to comprehend and recognize people (Fatt & Howe, 2003). He also defines it as a person's capability to comprehend other people's emotions and to implicate in adaptive social relationships. Roots of EI are also found in Gardner's Theory of Multiple Intelligences (1983) while the word 'Emotional Intelligence' was first used by Payne (1985) in his thesis, "A Study of Emotion: Developing Emotional Intelligence; Self-Integration; Relating to Fear, Pain, and Desire".

Complete and inclusive picture of the term EI was portrayed by Salovey and Mayer (1990) under the umbrella of Interpersonal and Intra-Personal Intelligence. Dr. Reuven Bar for the first time introduced the terminology 'Emotional Quotient' (EQ) in 1985, which was further, endorsed and popularized by Daniel Goleman in 1995. He defines, "EI as an individual's knowledge of his feelings and to make accurate decisions based on that knowledge." There are currently three main hypothetical models of EI. Mayor and Salovey's (1997) four branched ability model of EI, Goleman's EQ model which has four main paradigms: Self-Awareness, Self-

Regulation, Social Awareness and Relationship Management (Goleman, 1998). While the Bar-On Model defines EI as unified and interconnected emotional and social capabilities and competencies that leave a remarkable impact on intelligent behavior (Bar-on & Handley, 2003a).

1.2   Introduction

The idea of EI depends on the possibility that feelings and perceptions give a base to one another (Mesquita & Frijda, 1992; Scherer, 1997b). EI includes a person's capacity to perceive, comprehend, oversee and express feelings in a capable, successful, talented and healthier way in the work environment (Palmer & Stough, 2002). After the presentation and advancement of the idea of EI, it has been progressively adjusted and grasped by the universe of business and afterward by scholastics and educational institutions. EI abilities have been connected with leadership skills, fulfilling individual educational encounters, success and achievement in the working environment. It was understood over time that not only IQ was enough to expect better performance, but that IQ, along with EQ, was a solid indicator of effective and powerful performance in the work environment (Goleman, 1995, 1998; Bar-On, 2001; Nelson et al., 2005). It is assumed that EI has an initial role in the achievement and effectiveness of an individual at his working place (Stein, Book & Kanoy, 2013; Coetzee & Jansen, 2007).

This has brought about the requirement to mix up the EI proficiencies in scholarly curricula (Abraham, 2006). Teachers are considered as primary mainstays of the educational institutions. Educators teach the students building up their social understanding, awareness and inspirational mentalities. They have an incredible and prominent job in the personality development of a child. Recently, the idea of the EI has been progressing among educators in the learning situations, because of its incredible prominence. Teachers' personalities have a great role in affecting the reasoning and critical thinking abilities of learners (Isen, 1993). It likewise can impact teachers' self-adequacy beliefs (Chan, 2004; Drew, 2006; Penrose, Perry & Ball 2007). As indicated by Anderson (2004) EI can influence convictions about teaching, which alternatively influence teaching-learning process. Mendes (2003), Hasket and Bean (2003), and Hwang (2007) noted that an educator is a successful instructor if he has knowledge about his feelings and can manage it as per demand of the circumstances.

Goleman (1995), Hwang (2007), and Mucciolo et al., (2008) found teaching adequacy as educators' administration skills, leadership, availability for students, empathy and ability to inspire students. Sutton and Wheatly (2003) have expressed that the emotional competency of instructors is critical, both for their prosperity and for the excellent learning process in the classroom, as well as for the social and emotional advancement of learners. Instructors with better EI can confront clashes in a better way and can have better relationships. They are great at critical thinking and basic leadership skills (Hargreaves & Fullen, 1998; Anderson, 2004).

Instructors with great EI are adequately hopeful, adaptable, helpful, certain, confident, persuading, leading, friendly, enthusiastic, and able to work for development (Mortiboys, 2013). Teaching outcomes (Flander & Simon, 1969) enhanced teaching performance (Anand, 1983) the connection among educator and understudies (Walsh & Maffei, 1994; Carson, 1993; Boyd. et al., 2005) the capacity to spur students academics and confidence (Salami, 2010) individual attention (Mucciolo, Jahangiri, Choi & Spielman, 2008) mastery over the subject and compassion (Boyd et al., 2005), productive and healthy relationship abilities, critical thinking and the problem solving skills (Ming, 2003) time, outrage and stress management (Fabio & Palazzeschi, 2009;

Powell & Powell, 2010) are some of the ground-breaking pointers of educators' viability which are extremely emotional in nature.

The phase of Higher Secondary School is pervasive in learners' life, as at this stage new vistas open in front of the students. Teachers at this stage must be effective in preparing students for their future jobs. Teachers' job has turned out to be increasingly critical as he/she gives direction, guiding and motivating students for their professional improvement, but EI is the unrecognized segment of successful teaching (Mortiboys, 2005). However the encouraging learning process is not limited to the transfer of information, it also involves managing nervousness and anxiety, and imbues the classrooms with rush or energy (Claxton, 1999).Teachers' EI is ignored and not much- explored zone in Pakistan. Some work has superficially explored EI in recent times, overviewing instructors' EI and their teaching viability, the effect of EI on performance of the college teachers (Ismail & Idris, 2009) the effect of EI on the performance of educators in higher educational institutions (Delaney, Johnson, Johnson & Treslan, 2010). Numerous researchers have examined different factors that can comprise EI, for example, educators' EI and adapting techniques among college instructors (Bibi et al., 2015) teachers' healthy and productive relationship (Bhatti, 2009), conflict resolution methodologies in schools (Basit et al., 2010; Siraj Ud Din et al., 2011) EI and employees' performance (Chaudhry & Usman, 2011) work fulfillment and organizational commitment of educators (Chughtai & Zafar, 2006; Malik, Nawab, Naeem & Danish, 2010) productive relationship of educators (Shah, 2012) effect of non-verbal correspondence and teaching performance (Butt, 2011) students' behavior management (Baig, 2011) and professional pride and self-esteem of educators (Mushtaq, Shakoor, Azeem & Zia, 2012; Tabassum & Ali, 2012). Emotional Competency of an educator is significant for learning process and for socio-emotional advancement of students (Ramana, 2003). High EI of educators prompts high job fulfillment and achievement in their professional life (Hassan et al., 2015).

Keeping in view the idea of instructing and attributes of successful instructors which are exceptionally emotional, vague, ambiguous, huge, not well defined, clarified and characterized in different ways, by various researchers and educational scientists; TE will be assessed on the criteria of emotional and professional characteristics by the specialist. While keeping in view the above discussion, researchers' comprehension of EI is people's emotional mindfulness, emotional self-control and relationship abilities/skills. The above explanation is propelled and built on Goleman's model of EI.

1.3   Conceptual Framework of the Study

A Conceptual framework is a model that includes the key concepts of the research study that are used to understand the research concepts and the relationship between and among these concepts. The Conceptual Framework is used as a lens to make sense of the main theme of the research. The conceptual framework of current research is mainly inspired by Goleman's mixed model of EI (Goleman, 2006) which outlines four basic paradigms of EI i.e. self-awareness, self-management, social-awareness and social-skills. The said model further consists of twenty emotional competencies.

After analyzing common themes of EI and different models of EI, mainly of Goleman's model of EI, three main constructs of EI i.e. emotional self-awareness, emotional self-regulation and interpersonal skills are taken as leading competencies of teacher recognized as an emotionally intelligent teacher for the proposed research.

While after studying detailed investigation about teacher effectiveness three dimensions of teaching have been taken into consideration to explore their association and linkage with teachers' EI. The selected dimensions of TE are Teaching and Pedagogical Skills (TPS), Classroom Management Skills (CMS), Relationship Management Skills (RMS). So, the framework is comprised of six (06) concepts. Three (03) of these concepts are related to EI skills and three (03) characteristics are related to TE. Researchers have related EI to daily life and effectiveness at the workplace in diverse kinds and level of occupation and organization. According to Hanif (2004) positive emotions help to reduce the conflicts, improving the efficiency and performance of an individual. Studies have proved that teacher's effectiveness in the classroom has its traces of the constructs of EI as classroom management, teaching and pedagogical skills, knowledge of individual differences, problem-solving skills and motivational inspiration. Teacher trait of his content and pedagogical skills includes all characteristics linked with the delivery of class lessons, better teaching-learning process, student's enhanced achievement, quality engagement of students in their academic work. The concept of classroom management includes the physical, psychological, and socio-cultural environment of the student, as well as the ways and strategies adopted to manage the teaching-learning process. For better performance of students a teacher needs to use classroom management skills to effectively manage students behavioral and challenging problems of class-room with emphasis on students cognitive performance, psychological wellbeing, disruptive behavior and effective relationships (Fernandez et al., 2008). Classroom management is teacher's activities that help in developing an environment for improved socio-emotional and academic learning. Teachers having the ability to manage their emotions can effectively manage their classrooms as well as students' behavior and increased students' performance (Leedy & Smith, 2012). McLean and Connor (2015) revealed that classroom management also includes managing socio-emotional problems of the students. Lewis (1999) claimed that maintaining classroom discipline and managing personal and student's behaviour requires high EI. Further studies by Jadhav and Patil (2010) emphasized the importance of teachers' EI and their behavior management skills in enhancing and improving students' academic and behavioral product. Relationship management is how a teacher copes with relationship challenges and deal with it effectively, while the concept of motivating classroom environment deals with the teacher's encouraging and motivating behavior, his interactive and positive approach and attitude towards his students. TE is also mirrored in his/her capability to motivate students to think critically (Rani & Porgio, 2010).

Teaching nowadays is a challenging job which requires a teacher to be emotionally intelligent enough to cope with stress and conflicts, for effective communication and healthy relationship with other teachers, students, parents and administrators (Campbell & Ntobedzi, 2007). This trait of the teacher is concerned with how effectively he/she can cope a stressful conditions and do not let the stress affect his/her teaching in the classroom.

Keeping in view these studies, and hypothesis of this research, the conceptual framework of the study is as follows.

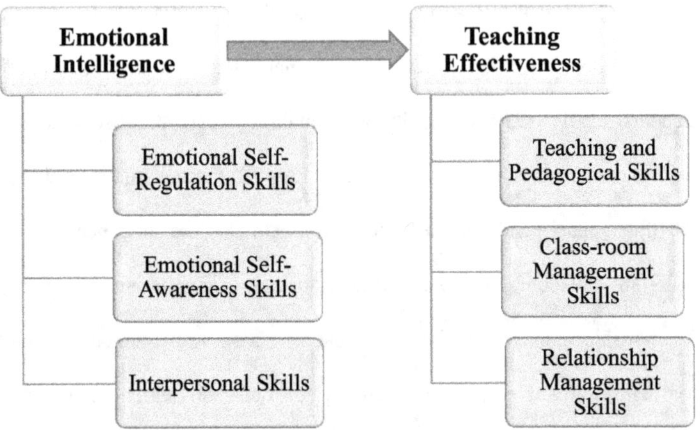

Conceptual framework of the study

1.4   Statement of the Problem

Despite the advancement and reforms in education and technology, the educational institutions still face challenges and issues such as distressing learners academic performance, declining interests of students in academic excellence, monumental demands and expectations of parents and society, underprivileged education system, workload of teachers and students etc. Such hurdles make it difficult for teachers to manage and cope with the academics, societal and social challenges and stressors. Teachers' inability to cope with these challenges result in emotional disturbances. Ignat and Clipa (2012) concluded that teachers with emotional competencies and skills can cope with these challenges easily and effectively. Here, the teacher's EI plays an important role in the effective management of their emotions. Numerous Researches on EI have recognized the importance of EI in improved performance at the job place. However, still work is needed on finding the significance of EI in the education sector. Teachers' role in the education system is very challenging and it requires the teacher to equip himself/herself with so many abilities and skills. One such fundamental skill of the teacher is his EI. The purpose of the proposed study is the analysis of teachers' EI and its impact on teaching effectiveness at higher secondary level in Khyber Pakhtunkhwa (KP).

1.5   Objectives of the Study

The study aims to

i.   Find out the teachers' Emotional Self-Regulation Skills and their impact on teaching effectiveness at the higher secondary level in Khyber Pakhtunkhwa.

ii.   Analyze teachers' Emotional Self-Awareness Skills and their impact on teaching effectiveness at the higher secondary level in Khyber Pakhtunkhwa.

iii.   Examine the teachers' Interpersonal Skills and their impact on teaching effectiveness at the higher secondary level in Khyber Pakhtunkhwa.

iv.   Determine the parameters of teaching effectiveness of teachers at the higher secondary level in Khyber Pakhtunkhwa.

v.   Investigate the effect of teachers' EI on their teaching effectiveness at the higher secondary level in Khyber Pakhtunkhwa.

1.6   Hypotheses of the study

The hypotheses of the study are

i.   There is no significant relationship between teachers' Emotional Self-Regulation Skills and Teaching Effectiveness.

ii.   There is no significant relationship between teachers' Emotional Self-Awareness Skills and Teaching Effectiveness.

iii.   There is no significant relationship between teachers' Interpersonal Skills and Teaching Effectiveness.

iv.   There is no significant relationship between teacher's demographic variables (gender, marital status, age and qualification) and EI.

v.   There is no significant relationship between EI of teachers and their Teaching Effectiveness.

1.7   Significance of the Study

The primary function of education is the inducement of the potentials and capabilities of a child and cultivates the skills in them to meet and encounter the challenges of life. Proper education of the child will help him/her understand the society and proper adjustment with his/her surroundings. After parents at home, a teacher is a person who molded the personality of a child. The personality of a child is largely mold and fashioned by the experiences, knowledge and talent of the teachers. The teacher in this regard needs to be well equipped in order to accomplish this great mission of shaping child's personality. The teacher has the responsibility of enabling and equipping the child to absorb values, building his/her personality, realize and polish the hidden inner qualities to tackle the challenges of life. Proper training is to be given so that the vacuum created by the modern world could be filled up by the enthusiasm, interest and desire to shoulder social responsibilities. The modern world has entered the age of rapid and drastic changes in science and technology. There is a growing competition in all walks of life among human beings. Humanity is trying to compete with modern technological accessories as well as cope with competition among fellow human being. As a result, there is emotional disturbance and turmoil in their lives. So emotional stability is the dire need of the day in the area of education industry.

According to Bolton (1969) if the purpose of education is to prepare a child for the progressing and developing world, then it is an indispensable characteristic of an effective teacher to be aware of the realities of the modern world. Therefore 'School Teachers' have a great role in molding future generation. Further they need to be emotionally intelligent, creative and effective in their performance. The seed for reaching the state of success is being sown in the initial stages of child schooling while the seed for promoting potential is sown by the higher secondary school teachers. Subsequently, the specialist needs to look at the impact of EI on educators' execution at higher auxiliary 'school teachers' to trace the validity of the seeds sown in the initial stage and at the higher secondary schooling.

Some work is currently in progress aims to discover the effect of EI, yet they overlook its significance and the case is especially true of Pakistani educators. As through discussion, it has been inferred that EI assumes a noteworthy job in various parts of the instructor's effective expert life. The proposed examination will move and gives a phase to discover trial signs to investigate the association between the EI of educators and its effect on their instructing viability. Besides, this investigation will give knowledge to organizers and arrangement creators about the changing requests of instructing and along these lines by and large encouraging learning procedure might be subjectively streamlined. This examination will likewise move the showing assessment criteria. The proposed examination will likewise help the rehearsing instructors to think about their qualities and shortcomings and will assist them with improving the ideal zones of educating adequacy.

1.8   Delimitation of the Study

Due to time and financial constraints the study was delimited to

   i.   Government higher secondary schools of the Kohat, Mansehra, Peshawar, Mardan, Malakand, Swat and Lakki Marwat districts.

ii.   All male and female teachers and students of government higher secondary schools of the mentioned districts.

iii.   Teachers of selected subjects i.e. Chemistry, Biology, Physics, Islamic history, Civics and Urdu literature.

iv.   Session 2016-17

1.9   Operational Definition

i.   **Emotional Intelligence (EI):** EI is a learned ability of an individual to identify, perform, comprehend, recognize and express emotions in a productive, creative and healthy way. EI is an individual's competency or ability to understand and appreciate his emotions along with understanding the emotions of others, and handle them effectively in a way that can help in building healthy and productive social relationships (Low & Nelson, 2004).

ii.   **Teaching Effectiveness (TE):** An effective teacher can bring out the desired result of teaching-learning process. TE involves excellent student teacher's healthy relationship with students and colleagues, supportive and compassionate classroom atmosphere, content and pedagogical skills, classroom management skills, awareness of child psychology and certain personality traits of a teacher as a result of teachers' EI.

iii.   **Teaching and Pedagogical skills:** It is concerned with teacher knowledge and delivery of his subject with a variety of teaching techniques. Content knowledge and pedagogical skills of the teacher are assumed to heighten the rate of academic progress of students (Darling-Hammond, 2000).

iv.   **Classroom Management.** Teacher ability to effectively and efficiently manage the classroom, teacher skills and strategies being used to keep classroom environment well organized, keep things and students behavior in order, motivated, alert, focused, and work for academic excellence during a class. Classroom management is the process of creating an atmosphere help to induce disciplined and healthy behavior in a classroom setting. The main objective behind executing classroom management skills is to reduce or eliminate the chances of troublesome behaviors and to enhance and promote student academic involvement (McLean & Connor, 2015). Teacher's positive attitude towards students, Encouraging behavior, emotionally secure environment, enthusiastic and energetic class-room, teacher humorous attitude, motivating and supporting learning environment all collectively comprise motivating and facilitating class room environment.

v. **Relationship Management:** Relationship and bond develop between teacher and student as an outcome of loving and caring attitude, support and fairness on the teacher's part. Teachers who have an intimate, optimistic, encouraging, helpful and compassionate bond with their students have capabilities to motivate their students to achieve higher, and show the best academic results. The relationship management skill of a teacher has positive and long-lasting effects on students' academic as well as social development (Cooper & Sawaf, 1997).

vi. **Higher secondary school:** The Higher Secondary schools means Intermediate Colleges in Pakistan. Students, who passed their Secondary School Certificate (SSC) examination, are promoted to higher classes i.e. first year and second year of the First year in Arts (FA), the First year in Science (F.Sc) to appear for Higher Secondary Examination (HSC). Students at Higher Secondary schools have two broad academic options i.e. Science and non-science (humanities) programs. Science branch (FSC includes Pre-Engineering, Premedical and Computer Science (referred to as Science General). Major subjects at F.Sc are Physics, Chemistry, Biology, Mathematics English and Computer Science while students going for another option or streamline are called FA or humanities group; major subjects include political science, civics, education, literature and many more.

vii. **Impact:** The oxford English dictionary defines the word impact 'marked effect or influence'. The word impact, influence and effect are often listed in dictionaries as synonyms for each other. The word impact in this research can be described as expected effect.

CHAPTER-2

REVIEW OF RELATED LITERATURE

The purpose of this chapter aims to reconnoiter the link and interdependence between teachers' Emotional Intelligence and its impact on their Teaching Effectiveness. This dissertation involves two main variables i.e. EI and TE. The facets of the two mentioned variables of the study is discussed below.

"Intelligence is an ability of an individual to think reasonably, act decisively and deal accordingly with an environment in an effective way" (Goleman, 1998; p-12).According to Sternberg (1999) Intelligence is an individual's ability to achieve significant goals. Song et al., (2010) views' of intelligence revolves around the transaction of analytical, practical, and creative aspects of the mind. According to them it is the ability of utilizing one's abilities to solve problems or adapt to the environment.

As a strong promoter for unconventional views of intelligence Sternberg (1999) assimilated a pearl of new word wisdom into his work called as Kaleidoscope Project. This project encourages updating college admission criteria to go beyond traditional academic standards and look at candidates' skill as wisdom, creativity, and practicality.

This is a universal fact that IQ tests measure the analytical and verbal aptitude of an individual, but this is also a fact that these IQ tests cannot measure creativity, practical performance, and problem-solving skills. The human mind functions in three ways: cognition, affect and motivation. Human cognition and affect when combine to work together give base to EI. The idea of EI finds its roots in Thorndike's ideas of intelligence, who defines social intelligence as an individual ability to understand people (as cited in Fatt & Howe, 2003). Thorndike (1920) also defines social intelligence that such an individual can recognize people, their emotional states and to get involved in adaptive social relations. According to Wechsler (1949) intelligence is a combination of "intellective" and "non-intellective" elements. According to him "non-intellective" elements of an individual intelligence were more significant for predicting a person's success in life. Non-intellective elements involve personal, emotional and social factors (Goleman, & Cherniss, 2001).

Darwin's most important work on the significance of expressing emotions for survival and existence gives rise to the formal history of EI (Hess & Bacigalupo, 2010). The earliest roots of EI also find its roots in the work of Charles Darwin on the importance of emotional expression. Till late 1900, conservative definitions of intelligence stressed over cognitive facets of intelligence i.e. recall, memory and problem-solving etc., but then revolutionary changes took place in the field of intelligence and researchers documented the significance of the non-cognitive facets of intelligence along with cognitive facets. Thorndike in 1920, used the word 'social intelligence' as a person's capability to know and get into others (Thorndike & Stein, 1937). David Wechsler in 1940 linked the words non-intellective factors with cognitive factors and stressed that intelligence cannot be fully defined without non-intellective or non-cognitive facets (Bar-On, 2004).

Howard Gardner in 1975, presented the notion of multiple intelligences which has incorporated both interpersonal and intrapersonal intelligence; the former one is related with an individual ability to comprehend the wishes, wants, intentions and motivation of people living in the outer world while the later on includes individual wisdom to understand and acknowledge person's strength, weaknesses, frights and motivation. Gardner was of the strong view that the two facets of intelligence i.e. inter and intrapersonal portray a complete picture of intelligence along with cognitive aspects (Smith, 2008). Although the same concept was being investigated from different aspects and was entitled differently, still it was the need of time to clarify and elaborate the term in detail and specify the missing half of the term 'intelligence'.

The term EI was first used by Wayne Payne in a doctoral dissertation entitled "A study of emotion: developing emotional intelligence; self-integration; relating to fear, pain and desire" (Payne, 1985). While the terminology of emotional quotient was first used by Keith Beasley in his article published in Mensa Magazine. "The development of a concept of psychological well-being" by Reuven Bar-On in 1988 was the first doctoral dissertation to use the term emotional quotient soon after its introduction (Bar-On & Parker, 2011). Soon after this dissertation, Peter Salovey and John Mayer publish an article namely "Emotional Intelligence" which became a milestone in the promotion of EI (Mayer & Salovey, 1997).

The concept of EI got the highest level of distinction shortly after the publication of Daniel Goleman's books including "Emotional Intelligence: Why it can matter more than IQ" and another one "Working with Emotional Intelligence" in the last decade of 20th century (Goleman, 2006). These publications brought a twist in the history and literature of an emotional twist. The idea of tying two concepts i.e. intelligence and emotions were pretty unique and innovative while first originated a couple of decades ago (Mayer, Salovey & Caruso, 2002).

2.1 Models of Emotional Intelligence

With a twist in the history of intelligence varying definitions and different models of EI have emerged. This increased awareness and information about cognitive intelligence and EI have created a considerable number of discrepancies and disagreements about the precise and correct meaning of this concept. Researchers tried to alter the definition, meanings and models of EI. Reuven Bar On previously discussed the concept as emotional and social intelligence in 1997, but later on continued with coining both terms as socio-emotional intelligence in 2006 (Bar On, 1997; Bar On, 2001). Mayer and Salovey (1997) also came up with enhanced definitions of EI. Danial Goleman originally presented his model of EI in 1998, but revised his model in 2000 (Goleman, 1998; Goleman & Cherniss, 2001). According to the Encyclopedia of Applied Psychology, three major theoretical models of EI has been recommended: the Mayer-Salovey model (Mayer & Salovey, 1997), the Goleman model (Goleman, 1998) and the Bar-On model (1997) (Moon, 2010).

2.1.1 The Mayer-Salovey Model

According to the Mayer-Salovey Model (ability model) of emotional intelligence defined EI as a subset of social intelligence that incorporates an individual's capability to understand one's feelings and emotions while understanding other people's emotions in more healthier way. They further mentioned that the same information can be applied to lead one's cognition and actions (Salovey & Mayer, 1990; Mayer, Salovey & Caruso, 2002).

Later on, the definition of EI was revised by Salovey and Mayer in the following words as

"Emotional intelligence involves an individual's ability to perceive, comprehend, and express emotions accurately; capability to accurately recognize feelings when they assist thought; the ability to understand emotional knowledge; and the ability to control and manage emotions to

*indorse and stimulate emotional and intellectual growth of an individual"(*Mayer & Salovey, 1997).

Mayer and Salovey revised the EI model which is comprised of four branches, organized hierarchically from more basic and simple psychological processes to more integrated and complex processes. People who lie high on this hierarchy are considered to have high EI and hypothetical to learn and progress faster than those who lie low on the hierarchy of EI.

Mayer and Salovey's Four Branched Model of EI

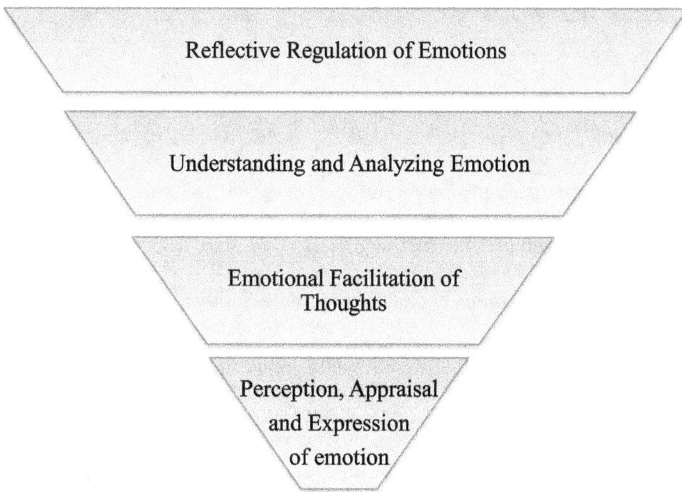

Figure 2.1.1: Revised Mayer-Salovey Model of EI 1997

Mayer, Salovey and Caruso (2000) regards EI as a set of interconnected capabilities and skills of an individual that allows him to process emotional information in more competent and accurate way. Each branch in this hierarchal model labels a set of individual's abilities that make up the overall EI of an individual. Each branch of this hierarchy has its developmental course, which proceeds from comparatively simple skills to more sophisticated and refined ones. The lowest level in this model explains how accurately a person can identify and recognize the emotions of himself and those of others and the pleasure related to these emotions and his ability to categorize the precise and imprecise way of expressing emotions. The next branch describes the intellectual processing of emotions. At this level an individual can recognize difficult and sophisticated emotions and understand a transition between different emotional states, while the top of this hieratical model is concerned with sensible emotional regulation to enrich and boost emotional and intellectual growth (Mayer & Salovey, 1997).

2.1.2   Daniel Goleman's Model of EI

Daniel Goleman's model also recognized as a Mixed Model of EI (Mayer, Salovey & Caruso, 2000). Goleman defined EI as "individual capability of identifying one's feelings and those of others, ability to motivate and manage emotions within himself and with people in his surroundings" (Goleman, 2004, p-317). His EI theory was being articulated in his book *"Working with Emotional Intelligence"* for the first time.

According to Daniel Goleman IQ only contributes 20% success in life, while 80% are factors other than IQ. (Goleman, 1995). He stated that IQ can interpret in the selection of people for different professions but success in different professions can be better predicted by EI (Goleman, 2001). Goleman's model has two versions, the old version contained five facets of EI and twenty-five socio-emotional skills.

Figure 2.1.2. a. Goleman Model of Emotional Intelligence (old version)

Personal skills	Self- awareness	Emotional consciousness
		Accurate self-assessment
		Self-assurance and confidence
	Self-regulation	Self-discipline
		Trust worthiness
		Carefulness/diligence
		Flexibility
		Innovation and novelty
	Motivation	Accomplishment drive
		Commitment
		Creativity
		Positivity
Social skills	Empathy	Understanding People
		Developing other
		Service orientation
		Leveraging diversity
		Political awareness
	Social skills	Encouragement
		Communication
		Leadership
		Conflict management
		Change promoter
		Building relationships
		Alliance and cooperation
		Team work competencies

Source: Goleman, (1998)

First three categories of this model lie in the intrapersonal domain while the last two belong to the Interpersonal domain. This model was revised in 2000 with some alterations and modifications, and the twenty-five EI skills were buckled into twenty, whiles the five domains were shrunk into four domains (Boyatzis, Goleman & Rhee, 2000).

Figure 2.1.2.b. Revised Model by Goleman

	Self	**Other**
	Personal Skills	**Social skills**
	Self-Awareness	Social Awareness
Emotional Recognition	Self-emotional knowledge and understanding	Empathy
		Coordination
	Precise self-assessment	Organizational teamwork knowledge
	Self-assurance and confidence	
	Self-Management skills	**Relationship Management skills**
	Self-control	Developing others
	Credibility	Inspiration and encouragement
Emotional Regulation	Thoroughness/carefulness	Communication
	Adaptability/flexibility	Conflict management
	Accomplishment drive	Leadership
	Creativity	Change promoter and facilitator
		Building relationships
		Teamwork & collaboration

Source: Goleman and Cherniss (2001)

This model appears to be influenced by the idea of social intelligence by Thorndike and Gardner's theory of intelligence.

2.1.3 The Bar-On Model

Bar-On model is the combination of different mental abilities and some personality traits, that's why it is also called as mixed model of EI as well (Mayer et al., 2000). EI can be considered as a set of interlinked socio-emotional skills of an individual which affects the means one identifies his/her emotions and express accordingly, developing and keeping healthy relationships, facing challenges, and using this information productively and effectively way. According to Bar-On Socio-Emotional intelligence is a series of several inter connected socio-emotional skills that regulates the way how we understand and express our emotions, comprehend feelings of others, keeping healthy relations with them, and face daily strains and pressures (Bar-On, 2004; Bar-On, & Parker, 2011). There are five key components and fifteen competencies of this model.

Figure 2.1.3. Bar on Model of Emotional- Social Intelligence Eq-I and Eq-I2

EQ-I		EQi-2	
Intrapersonal	- Self-regard - Self- actualization - Emotional self-awareness - Assertiveness - Independence	Self-perception	- Self-regard - Self-actualization - Emotional self-awareness
Interpersonal	- Interpersonal relationship - Empathy - Social responsibility	Self-expression	- Emotional expression - Assertiveness - Independence
Adaptability	- Problem-solving - Reality testing - Flexibility	Interpersonal	- Interpersonal relationships - Empathy - Social responsibility
Stress management	- Impulse control - Stress tolerance	Decision-making	- Problem-solving - Reality testing - Impulse control
General mood	- Optimism - Happiness	Stress management	- Flexibility - Stress tolerance - Optimism
		Well-being indicator	- Happiness

Source: Multi-Health Systems Inc. (2011)

2.2   Emotional Intelligence in Everyday Life

Emotions have a significant role in all spares of living (Bar On, 1997). While in the growing stages of our life we are being taught by our society in general and by our schools and parents in specific to think of emotions as an intellectual response rather than an emotional one. Even the term emotional is taken or perceived as a very negative and a weak trait of personality. We focus more on academic intelligence, completely ignoring and denying the significance of EI and think of the human being just as think tank who can only think but can't feel. Since the early ages of life a child is being taught to suppress his emotions as the best possible way of emotional management. Suppressing emotions and insufficient skills to manage and express emotions lead to psychological tensions. Some of the outcomes of mishandling and mismanagement of emotions are job dissatisfaction, stress, unhealthy relationships, frustration, anger and anxiety (Singh, 2003). Positive emotions play a dynamic and significant role in maintaining healthy life style, healthy inter and intra personal relations, and productive performance at work places, there always exist a positive relationship between emotional health and healthy interpersonal relationships (Lopes, Grewal, Kadis, Gall & Salovey, 2006; Parker et al., 2005; Singh, 2003). Emotional health also resulted in organizational commitment, job satisfaction, improved performance, effective and strong leadership (Zeidner, Matthews & Roberts, 2001; Singh, 2003) well-being and healthy personality of an individual (Donaldso-feider & Bond, 2004) productive emotional regulation, thinking clarity and psychological well-being (Edward, 1973;Schutte, Malouff & Hine, 2011) social coping (Chan, 2004;2008) healthy social skills, cooperation, interpersonal relations, marital satisfaction (Schutte et al., 2009) and overall satisfaction and healthy lives (Palomera, Fernandez-Berrocal, Brackett, 2008; Law, Wong et al., 2018; Palmer, Donaldson &

Stough, 2002; Singh,2008) while unhealthy or negative emotions leads to examination stress and anxiety (Austin, Saklofske, & Egan, 2005) disproportionate use of alcohol, illegal drugs, and deviancy (Brackett, & Katulak, 2006; Stein, Book, & Kanoy, 2013) work stress (Chang, 2006) domestic violence anxiety and depression (Baker & Berenbaum, 2007), and hitches in making decision (Fabio, & Palazeschi, 2009). EI even help employees resolve their conflicts (both external & internal), enable them to accomplish and achieve their goals, improve memory, decision making skill and clarity of thinking (Singh, 2015). There are innumerable examples in the real field of business, politics and academics, successful people in professional fields with low IQ level (Singh, 2015).

2.3   Importance of Emotions in Teachers' Life

Where there are people, there will be a display of a variety of the emotions; same is true for educational institutions (Hargreaves, 1998). According to GU and Day (2007) teaching is a field which does not require teachers merely with healthy cognition, but also healthy emotional states as they come up not only with 'the head' but also with 'the heart'. It means educational institutions do not only display cognitive setting, but the emotional setting as well. Unfortunately we value head and devalue heart, though our professional success is mostly determined by our emotional health (Singh, 2015).

List of careers generally requiring from lowest to highest EI

Lowest

Botanist

Biochemist

Chef

System analyst

Engineer

Auditor

Accountant

Banker

Judiciary

Banker

Editor

Manager

Travel agent

Civil servant

Librarian

Writer

Doctor

Police officer

Training manager

Artist

Human resource manager

Business persons

Politics

Teachers

Social workers

Psychiatrist/ psychologist

Highest

Figure 2.3.1 Why Teachers is required to be Emotionally Intelligent?

Source: Singh (2003)

The table shows clearly the importance and significance of EI skills for the teaching profession. Teaching is a skill that requires high professional, academic and emotional skills. EI helps teachers better accommodate themselves in their workplace. Teaching is declared as an intensely emotional work process, which involves a blend of all emotions from joyfulness to anger (Hargreaves, 1998). Teaching is a job where he/she has to wear many hats according to the need and demands of the existing situation. Sometimes a teacher will have to play the role of a friend, sometimes protector, mentor, and disciplinarian, while at another time gatekeeper for students' academic success (Davis & Wilson, 2000). These different roles played by teachers as professionals makes their life more complex. It is a tense job as it requires handling complex relations, deal with people of different nature (knowledge of individual differences), highly complex objectives and goals to achieve, and insufficient time to achieve those goals may cause their emotional burn out. To perform all these roles of a teacher they need to be emotionally intelligent, which helps them better deal with all these stressors (Kim, 2002).

Chang (2006) argues that emotional labor, knowledge and understanding is more important for a teacher as compare to other professions. Emotional management and regulation have a positive impact on teacher's performance (Palomera, Fernandez-Berrocal & Brackett, 2008). To effectively deal with complex social relations, teachers' emotional skills are as significant as their intellectual and cognitive energy (Davis & Wilson, 2000, GU & Day, 2007).

In their study Sutton and Wheatley (2003) and Sutton (2004) in their study declared few emotional states that have positive effects over teachers' performance as love, passion, hope and satisfaction. They also added that these positive emotions resulted in a healthy interpersonal relationship, students' greater achievement, motivate them to struggle, initiate positive responses, teacher availability for students during and after their academic time, and greater sense of responsibility. They also reported that harmful emotions like guilt, anger, anxiety and teachers' frustration leads to unaccomplished objectives, behavioral and disciplinary problems in the classroom, unhealthy relationship and under achievement of students.

In this epoch of rapid growth and globalization, it is mandatory to encourage and promote an individual's emotional skills, along with cognitive skills to produce well-balanced personalities. Pakistan's National Education Policy (2009) clearly highlighted that education is regarded as a Source worthy sponsor of "attainment of social goals, promoting civic responsibility, social solidity, and more tolerant and broadminded society" (p.55). It reflects that education does not only emphasis on (a) fabrication of skilful labor and (b) generation of knowledge and cognitive development but also (c) to prepare the productive individuals for the service of society, who are more tolerant towards the changing tasks and challenges of life and society by inculcating in them socio-emotional skills (National Education Policy, 2009).The role of the teacher is continuously changing and increasing keeping in view the needs and demands of national and international challenges. Specifically the arising scenarios in Pakistan where there is an increased number of evidence of higher students' aggression rate, violence, intolerance, frustration and hopelessness. Now it's need of the time for a teacher to adapt himself according to the changing demands and needs of students and society as a whole.

Thus, today's teacher role is becoming more difficult and demanding (William & Burden, 2000). Their jobs require them to work under continuous stress and pressure. Teachers hold a central position in any education system. They are role models for students as they are being observed and followed by their students. In crux, the dream of social solidity is possible only if their teachers are well versed with cognitive, intellectual, professional, and socio-emotional skills.

2.4   Teaching Effectiveness

"Teaching effectiveness is the product of the continuous support of both the head (cognition) and the heart (emotion) to each other" (GU and Day, 2007; p-1302).According to Doyle (2012) TE is *"the amount of student learning occurs in the class room"* (p-2). It is the process of creating possibilities for student's learning, discussion and participation opportunities which will ultimately lead to their intellectual and academic success (Aregbeyen, 2010).

Educational organizations are believed as the most prominent foundation for students' academic development and competence. In these academic institutions teachers have the major responsibility to guarantee, the information is properly being conveyed and understood by students. Another prominent duty of a teacher is to make sure that the course and syllabus are being covered and completed in time. Besides, the teacher also plays a pivotal role in maintaining classroom discipline, managing better and healthy interaction with students, effective interaction with parents and other stakeholders of educational institutes.

Classroom management is regarded as the most prominent aspect of TE (Berliner, 1983; Brophy & Good 1992). Rubin (1984) describes the knowledge of individual differences and respect for diversities as a significant feature of effective teaching. Brophy (1983) concentrated on the utilization of motivational tools by teacher, interpersonal relationships, and commitment as an important factor for the effective teaching process. It was indicated by Fullen and Hargreaves (1992) that teacher knowledge and command over subject is a great contributor towards his teaching efficiency and effectiveness. Lunerbrug (1996) described an effective teacher role as a guide and counsellor, who is available and approachable for students to solve their problems in and out of their academic settings. Some of the traits of effective teaching were found as kindness, empathy, knowledge, communication skills, organized learning material, ability to motivate and inspire learners, friendly nature, classroom management skills, confidence, leadership, and self-esteem (Hwang, 2007). Every Single class room is a blend or combination of students having different intellectual levels and different cultural, religious and ethnic backgrounds with different mind sets. Here TE is concerned with the teacher's knowledge of individual differences, accepting and appreciating those differences and diversities and can transfer this tolerance among his students by role modeling. According to Rubin (1984) an effective teacher always focus on providing individual attention to all students.

The literature collected about the traits of an effective teacher concluded that an effective teacher has skills like subject command, clarity and instructional skills (Hargreves, 1998; Motriboys, 2005; Powel & Kusuma-Powel, 2010), healthy interpersonal relationship (Hargreves, 1998) and effective communication abilities (Thomas, 2008). An effective teacher is helpful (Miller, 2010) kind, adaptable, active, energetic, flexible, focused, trustworthy, consistent, stable, always ready for experimentation (Mortiboys, 2013) humble, compassionate, empathetic, helpful, know students emotionally, recognizes and appreciates students learning needs (Coetzee &Jansen, 2007). He/she can make his class room a pleasant, artistic, tough, joyous and interesting for learning (Hargreves, 1998; Powel & Kusuma-Powel, 2010) he/she is passionate and eager to learn and convey new things (Hargreves, 1998; Mortiboys, 2005). He/she readily involve himself in students' academics and performances and play a role in inducing them to do more (Nelson, Low, & Nelson,

2005) and also supports students' ideas, has strong class room management skills (Powel & Kusuma-Powel, 2010; Wilson & Corbet, 2002) practices humor to make his/her leaning process more interesting (Cotzee & Jansen, 2007; Mortiboys, 2005) has expectations towards students within their cognitive and emotional differences (Powel & Kusuma-Powel, 2010) and work to heighten the students' performance (Powel & Kusuma-Powel, 2010). He/she helps students accomplish their tasks and achieve their goals (Wilson & Corbett, 2002). Brophy (1983) mentioned that an effective teacher has the strength to keep students motivated and enthusiastic to learn new things and excel in academic performance. In addition, the teacher's personality, self-reliance, confidence, relationship with other stakeholders (students, parents, colleagues) and his/her ability to motivate students to make him/her a perfect teacher (Jahangiri, Mucciolo, Choi & Spielman, 2008).

In his research, Feldman (1999) explored few characteristics of teachers that are being admired by their students. According to those students effective teachers know their teaching objectives, command over their subject and content, ability to raise students' interest, effective communication skills, knowledge of child psychology and individual differences, can teach students keeping in view all the differences, appropriate knowledge of the subject, use audio-visual aids tactfully, class room management skills, provide their pupils with on-time feedback, appreciate discussion, initiate challenging classroom atmosphere, show reverence towards their students, are passionate about their profession, highly intellectual, organized, have a clear vision, do a fair assessment, co-operative and are always ready for students help and counselling and have ability to inspire students.

Teaching is regarded as one of the most demanding and stress full professions, as it involves social interactions with different stakeholders where they should very often regulate their own emotions as well as of their students, parents and colleagues (Brotheridge & Grandey, 2002). Positive emotions may facilitate a suitable climate for teaching (Sutton & Whealey, 2003). However, a high level of stress and negative emotional reactivity cause burn-out (Mendes, 2003). Teachers consciously and unconsciously display emotions that can significantly enhance or inhibit student teaching (Powell & Powell, 2010). Based on Daniel Goleman's five components of EI, Powell and Powell (2010) stated that self-awareness, self-regulation, motivation, social awareness, and relationship management can help increase TE in the classroom.

TE is all about teachers' knowledge of curriculum, content and pedagogy, teacher's behavior and skills that can motivate students to learn and improved intellectual performance (Medley & Coker, 1987; Olson, Mc Cubbin, Barnes, Muxen, Larsen, & Wilson, 1989). A competent teacher is variably warm and pleasant, has a clear set of objectives, implements precisely whatever is planned, has effective management, presentation, and communication skills, capable of motivating students and give individual attention to students (Gupta & Kaur, 2006).

As we expect individual differences amongst our students in a classroom setting, we also expect individual differences amongst teachers in their skills and abilities. Each teacher is unique in his/her skills, abilities and competencies. These differences are the result of their education, their teaching experiences, educational and cultural differences they belong to. These differences will have an impact on their skills, competencies, motivation, commitment and engagement. Qualter, Whitely, Morley and Dudiak (2009) noted that effective teachers are caring, helpful and have command over their subject. TE includes knowledge of the subject matter, content and methodology, effective communication skills, ability to inspire students, healthy relationships and classroom management skills.

According to Robert (1996) Teacher's performance is the extent of teacher's mastery over the subject matter, self-reliance, regularity, confidence, emotional flexibility, productive interpersonal relationships with students and colleagues, effective communication skills, planning and groundwork, task orientation and assessment. Teacher personality correlates with his/her performance which leads to their TE (Wool fork, Hughes & Walkup, 2008).

Carmeli and Josman (2006) divided teaching skills into two broad classes' i.e. pedagogical skills and professional skills. They further develop parameters of TE i.e. content and pedagogical skills, class-room management, communication strategies, use of motivational tools, accepting and appreciating diversities, problem-solving and decision making skills etc. Some of the indicators of TE are effective communication, knowledge of individual differences, using a variety of teaching methodologies, promotes students positive growth etc. (Hwang, 2007).

A teacher's success is no doubt linked and associated with his/her intellectual ability. However, the latest studies have suggested that teacher's cognitive intelligence and experience is not the only indicator of teaching success and effectiveness but their teaching skills and competencies are indispensable and crucial elements to be a successful teacher. 21st Century demands a teacher to develop essential teaching skills and competencies. According to a report by Anderson (2004) an efficient teacher must have command and mastery of his/her subject. There are three main components of the education system i.e. curriculum, student and teacher. Among these three components the teacher is the most important and crucial element as he/she is responsible for the effective delivery of the curriculum and responsible for all the elements related to the student learning process. The entire curriculum and the objectives of that curriculum are being translated by one of the main components of the education system and that is the teacher. So his teaching competency and skills are the utmost requirement of an education system to translate and deliver this curriculum most desirably and effectively.

The foremost objective of all the educational institutions at all stages is the attainment of student's academic excellence and success. There are certain other educational objectives as mentioned in Pakistan's educational policies time and again i.e. personality development, moral, social, and cultural development. Achievement of these goals is carried out by a work force called teachers. It is a known fact that people of any country are the inflated copy of their teachers. Teachers are the real nation builders. They have the fate of the nation in their hands. They can build or destroy the nation. They have the responsibility to educate the nation and build their future, to make their lives progressive, cultured and civilized. So the term teaching is defined as a set of observable teacher behaviors that facilitate or bring about the desirable short-run and long-run outcomes. EI can guide teachers to develop a strong and communicative relationship with their colleagues and students. They can avoid conflicting situations and may have a better solution for problems with the help of EI skills. The following are some of the characteristics or traits of teachers that are linked with their TE.

Figure 2.4.1 Teachers' Characteristics Linked with Their Effectiveness

Cluster	Characteristics	Description
Professionalism	i. Commitment ii. Confidence iii. Trustworthiness iv. Respect	i. Commitment to do every possible thing for students success ii. Ability to take on challenges iii. Consistent and fair iv. Respect all kinds of diversities
Thinking/ reasoning	i. Analytical/Conceptual thinking	ii. Ability to think logically, establishing cause and effect relationship
Expectation	i. Drive for improvement ii. Information seeking	i. Setting and meeting challenges and goals ii. Intellectual curiosity
Leadership	i. Flexibility ii. Accountability iii. Desire to learn	i. Adapting according to the needs and demands of the situation ii. Ability to set clear expectation and accountability to meet those expectations iii. Ability to make students confident and independent

Source: Adapted from McBer, (2000).

2.5   Need of Emotional Intelligence for Teaching Effectiveness

Our nation is standing at the threshold of the 21[st]Century and the quality of its citizen's lives depends on how effectively a nation can face internal and external challenges. For the said purpose education is considered as the most effective and desirable instrument to meet these challenges. Meaningful and productive education to meet the challenges successfully, we should take into account the needs and aspirations of society along with the physical and cognitive growth of individuals. The objectives and purposes of the education industry have dramatically changed due to changing expectations and the arising needs of society. Teacher personality is considered the most important component to achieve desired objectives of our education policies and the education system. Need of the time is not only to focus on the cognitive development of students, but the focus should be on the production of citizens who will positively contribute towards society, with social integration and cohesion by instilling and inducing in them certain socio-emotional skill (National Education Policy, 2009). However, if the teacher lacks certain socio- emotional skills, we cannot expect them to induce and inculcate these skills among students. They are considered as an agent of bringing these desirable changes amongst youth. We can inculcate social cohesion, integration and patriotism in our student community only if our teachers possess cognitive, professional, social and emotional skills (Chechi, 2012).

Amritha and Kadhiravan (2006) concluded that the Higher Secondary Stage is a very critical and significant stage of child's life in his education. At this stage the student is confronted with new vistas and ways in front of him. Due to the rapid increase and development of technology, as well as other emerging and arising issues a teacher must be effective to prepare his students for their future roles. Here the teacher plays the role of guide and counsellor and inspires students for their career development. The effectiveness of the process of education is rightly seen in the effectiveness of the teachers. To materialize educational policies and plans in a real sense, the education system needs effective teachers. Teacher performance and effectiveness matters a lot, which to a great extent is dependent on the EI and personality of the teacher. As it is believed that real changes do not happen from top-bottom, but real changes happen from the bottom up in the communities. Teachers are the real agents of bringing change in societies, their character, behavior and attitude have the power to mould child personality and character in the most desirable way.

It was revealed from the study of Titsworth, Quinlan and Mazer (2010), that Teachers have to play varying roles in their professional lives and their emotional health and intelligence can help them to perform all their roles and duties effectively. Teaching is a demanding job that requires dealing with people and their emotions, complex goals and objectives. Work load and scarce time for themselves may exhaust and frustrate the teachers. EI skills may help them deal with all these stressors in a better and effective way.

Goleman, (1995, 1998) and Bar On, (2001) quoted in their works that the notion of EI in the teaching-learning process is gaining a lot of attention and due consideration has been given to this phenomenon due to its great prominence. A person can understands one's own emotions and those of other people around, mean recognizing and managing feelings and emotions. Therefore, this proficiency is obligatory and of significant importance for effective teaching. EI contributes positively to individual's personal and   professional success in different fields of life. This is the reason that at the time of selection in the armed forces, psychological tests are used to assess entrants' traits, to select individuals with strong management skills, can manage and cope with the stress productively. Wilfully, teachers are considered as the builder of the forthcoming nation and are responsible for their overall development. When we intend to assign teachers for them, we do not keep into view the complete requirements and we only qualify   teachers with highest qualification and degrees among all the applicants. Recruitment nowadays done by a private company namely National Testing Service (NTS), is based solely on their cognitive intelligence, while

Teaching is not just a matter of subject command, but it is about efficiency, correct competencies and skills (Bibi, Kazmi, Chaudhry & Khan, 2015).

The role of the teacher is significant as teacher is the responsible to facilitate the psychological development of students along with their cognitive development. If the teacher can identify his/her own and students' emotional states, he/she will be having a profound understanding of the students' behaviour in different situations. On the other hand, the dearth of knowledge and understanding about the emotional states of self or others can heighten the problem of misinterpretation of behavior display and implementation of unsuitable tactics to handle such behaviors. EI is becoming a dominant factor for predicting teacher's effective performance in schools, colleges and universities (Jennings & Greenberg, 2009). The emotional competence of teachers can be better revealed in the form of a student's performance (Brackett & Katulak, 2006).Teachers that are unable to deal with their stressors at home also exhibit negative behaviour within the classroom, which resulted in the declined performance of a teacher, eventually resulting in the declined performance of the students.

The role of teachers is becoming more significant as they facilitate the psychological growth of students along with their cognitive and intellectual growth. Identification and knowledge of student's emotional states can generate a deeper understanding of student's behavior as to why they behave and react in certain situation. A teacher with no awareness of his emotional states will handle students' problematic behaviour in an inappropriate way (Jennings & Greenberg, 2009).

Teachers' EI is generally viewed as a means to enhance teachers' performance and efficiency. TE is comprised of healthy and productive teacher-student relationships, active and enthusiastic classroom condition, content and pedagogical skills, and classroom management skills. TE is also a teacher's trait of lesson planning and preparation, classroom and time management, command over the subject, interpersonal relationship, attitude towards children and use of audio-visual aids during their teaching-learning process. TE and teachers' EI has caught the researcher's attention few years back and is an emergent area of research.

Recently, researchers are working to investigate the role of emotions and EI as a means to improve work performance in educational settings (Sutton, 2004; Arnold, 2005; Jennings & Greenberg, 2009; Rohana, Kamaruzaman, & Zanariah, 2009; Najmuddin, Noriah, & Mohammad, 2011). EI can also predict a sense of contentment and performance at job place (Bachman, Stein, Campbell, & Sitarenios, 2000; Prati, Douglas, Ferris, Ammeter, & Buckley, 2003; Wong& Law, 2002). EI involves handling and understanding one's own emotions and those of others, motivation, empathy, and healthy interpersonal relationships (Goleman, 1995). EI is an individual ability to recognize, understand, manage and express emotions effectively and productively at job place. EI has been documented and acknowledged as a significant contributor to success at the workplace (Goleman, 1998; Parker et al., 2004).This acknowledgment has ensued the need for incorporating EI skills in schools curricula (Weisinger, 1998; Nelson, Low, Nelson, 2005).

EI is considered as an extremely common procedure, yet it tends to be enhanced, advanced, and can be scholarly. Goad (2005) and Justice (2005) likewise feel the centrality and worth of EI in educator's preparation and development programs. According to them EI should be a vital part of pre-service teacher education and training. The researchers viewed that teacher's EI contributes largely to the success of any educational program.

George (2000) focused on teachers, who are skilled in managing and handling emotions have healthy communication skills, can better accomplish and achieve their goals which results in effective performance. They are more empathetic towards other, available to provide emotional support and are more attentive to others' needs. The inability of an instructor to make a classroom domain that underpins the quick-paced and fast learning among learners in the class room can restrain the execution of the learners, while the educators' performance is linked with the nature of collaboration which has been set up with students. Keeping in mind these facts, the educational scientists have recommended the incorporation of training programs preparing for the advancement of the dimension of the emotional ability of teachers (Hawkey, 2006). Mesquita, Frijda & Scherer (1997) indicated that previous researches have proved that IQ alone cannot measure teachers personal and professional success, but EI is a vibrant and dynamic requirement to measure and assess his success and professional growth. It was claimed there existed a durable relationship between teachers' emotional traits and student's emotional growth, while there is a strong belief that emotions and cognitions supports each other.

According to Parker et al., (2003) knowing one's self is as necessary for a good teacher as knowing his students and the subject. Teachers act as the main pillar or the foundation of the education system. They are considered as the conveyer of knowledge to a new generation to make them unable to achieve their future goals. In classroom situation they have to connect with their students and they are teachers who can create a classroom environment that will stimulate pleasure, energy, creativity, and joy. Teachers daily have to face and connect with so many people involved in educational setting i.e. colleagues, administrators, parents and students daily. They also have to face heavy workload and pressures, while always in state to deal with disciplinary problems in the class room as well as dealing with other stakeholders (Brotheridge & Grandey, 2002).

Teachers EI influence their behavior, thinking style and problem-solving skills (Isen, 1993) also affect their beliefs about themselves (Chan, 2004; Drew, 2006; Penrose, Perry, & Ball, 2007). EI of a teacher can influence a teacher's convictions about his teaching, which paved the way for effective teaching and learning (Anderson, 2004). So, EI can influence a teacher's working behavior and success.

Chang (2006) suggested that EI of teachers' at their work place is more important than any other profession. Their EI may also help them with better adjustment in their workplace.

Teaching profession requires them to be innovative in their methodologies, attitude, flexibility, keeping them up to date with emerging knowledge in their fields, have knowledge of individual interests and need, respect and appreciate the diversities and can create an environment that will enhance and enlighten the environment for students development and progress. In crux, a successful teacher is one who is equipped with intellectual, socio-emotional and professional skills (Chechi, 2012).

Powell and Powell (2010) described and portrayed few characteristics of emotionally healthy teachers in the following way. Teacher who has high EI is;

    i.   Flexible and have a positive attitude towards any change (change management);

    ii.   Capable to solve problems effectively and proficiently even under pressure (decision making/stress management);

    iii.   Energetic and motivated to achieve goals (motivation);

    iv.   Capable of completing his responsibilities (time management/responsible);

v.   Calm in stressful situations (stress management);

vi.   Capable to cope effectively with anxiety and aggression (anxiety, stress and anger management);

vii.   Open towards diversities (tolerance);

viii. Effective in communication, has healthy and constructive relationships (healthy relations);

ix.   Ability to motivate and inspire people (leadership)

Successful professional whether they are in marketing, politics, teaching, or health requires high degrees of interpersonal intelligence (Goleman, 1995). It is believed that emotional competence of teachers is not only essential for their well-being but better teaching-learning processes as well. Teachers with improved EI have better communication skills, can resolve conflicts in a better way (Ming, 2003) are problem solvers, have high self-esteem, motivated, assertive, and responsible and can manage stress easily (Salami, 2010).

Teachers with high level of EI can perform better than others who are low on EI. Thus, it becomes obvious that teachers' emotional proficiency is indispensable, not for their well-being only but effective teaching, as well as for students' socio-emotional development (Sutton & Wheatly, 2003; Anderson, 2004). Di Fabio and Palazzeschi (2008) found that *"Higher EI was linked to higher teacher self-efficacy with high capacity of classroom management skills, high degree of motivation and students involvement while using appropriate teaching strategies"* (p-322).

Teachers with high EI establish relations with students and colleagues more successfully. They are confident, have more patience in relations with other people, more easily manage themselves, and more easily find ways to resolve their conflicts.

Emotionally literate teachers have better communication skills, ideas expressed are clearer and more appropriate to students' age, more relevant, simple, systematized; healthy interpersonal relationships, are more skilful listeners, they paraphrase students' statements better; more easily observe the problems in communication and develop a strategy and specific behaviors to overcome communication problems.Parameter for the success of any educational program is the level of teacher's EI and their competence (Katyal, & Awasthi, 2017).

Mendes (2003) conducted a study on "The relationship between emotional intelligence and occupational burnout among secondary school teachers" at Walden University, Minnesota, USA. Sample of the study comprised 49 secondary school teachers. Multifactor Emotional Intelligence Scale–MEIS was used to measure teachers EI, and Maslach Burnout Inventory-Educators Survey - MBI-ES to assess their burn-out level. Results of the study found that teachers' emotional exhaustion affect their ability to manage their emotions.

Hasket (2003) also postured the same question of whether there is any relationship between teacher's socio-emotional intelligence and their teaching performance among university teachers. 286 university teachers were selected as the sample size for the study. Scholars used EQ-i short to know about teachers' EI skills and seven principles to evaluate their teaching performance. Researcher discovered a strong link between teacher EI and their effectiveness.

Haskett & Bean (2003) study tried to explore the relationship between EI and teaching success in higher education. Sample of the study was 86 teaching award winners and 200 arbitrarily selected non-award teachers from higher institutions to compare their performance. EQ-i short was used to assess teachers' EI skills and "seven principles for good practice in undergraduate education" to measure their TE. Results pointed out a high relationship between EI skills and TE.

Pathan (2004) conducted a study to discover the level of teacher's EI at the secondary level, Navapur, Maharashtra. The study aimed to find the level of EI of secondary school teachers in relation to their gender and age. 'Emotional Intelligence Test' by Chadha and Singh (2001) was used to measure EI of teachers. Results of the study suggested that there is a significant difference between EI of male and female teachers, females performed better than their counterparts, while the study found age as independent of EI.

Todd (2006) was interested to find out whether teacher and students performance was having any linkage with emotional EI. His results suggested a positive relationship between EI and student and teacher performance.

Abraham (2006) indicated that it's teachers' responsibility to teach socio-emotional and technical skills to their students to promote in them leadership skills and well-rounded individuals.

Shah (2006) also conducted a study called "Emotional Intelligence of Upper Primary Students of Gujarat State in Relation to Certain Variables". Purpose of this study was to explore the association between EI concerning their gender, area, and socio-economic status. Study indicated that there was no significant difference in the mean scores on EI about gender, area, and socio-economic status of teachers.

Hwang (2007) also examined the relationships between the teachers' EI and TE. A convenient sampling method was adopted to select 94 teachers in Taiwan. The Exploring and Developing Emotional Intelligence Skills developed by Nelson et al.,

(2005) was used to assess EI of teachers. The study revealed a significant relationship between EI skills and TE.

Study findings of Penrose et al., (2007) suggested that EI can improve the TE which ultimately leads to enhanced students' performance.

Drew (2006) in his study tried to explore whether there is any relationship between Student Teacher Performance (STP) and Emotional Intelligence (EI). Researchers often use EQ-i to measure EI. Researcher found a positive and strong bond between overall EI with STP.

Di Fabio and Palazzeschi (2009) surveyed to examine the impact of EI with teacher competence. Study involved 169 high school teachers in Italy. Researchers found that EI is positively linked with teacher's self-efficacy beliefs, with higher classroom management skills, ability to motivate students, and adopting appropriate teaching strategies.

Ghanizadeh (2010) performed an examination to look at the relationship between teachers' EI and achievement in educational aptitudes. Eighty-nine (89) EFL teachers from Iran were selected as an example of the examination. Bar-On's EQ-I was utilized to quantify their EI. In the meantime, students of these teachers were required to fill the questionnaire 'Characteristics of successful teachers' to evaluate their teachers' performance. The examiner found a noteworthy connection between enhanced teachers' EI and their professional effectiveness.

Topno (2011) conducted an exploration to enquire about EI, teacher innovation and their effectiveness at elementary schools in India. Goal of the investigation was to build up a relationship between EI and TE. Random sampling technique was adopted to choose sample for the investigation from four districts of Bihar. 708 grade 05 teachers were selected as the sample of the study. The researcher used the tool designed by Anna raja and Thomas Perumalil (1980) and redesigned by Thomas Alexander in 2004. Examiner found a positive connection between teachers' EI and their effectiveness.

Lenka and Kant (2012) conducted a study to discover the relationship between teacher's emotional advancement and professional improvement. 120 teachers from secondary schools were being selected to examine the connection between teachers EI and professional advancement. They found a noteworthy connection between EI and professional development of teachers. They further included their examination that learning is a deep-rooted nonstop procedure which give base to individual and professional development of a teacher.

Jha (2012) found that EI affects the job performance of teachers at medical and engineering colleges. 250 teachers from 71 medical and engineering colleges of Uttar Pradesh, India were selected as a sample of the investigation. To quantify the extent of teachers EI, self-reported teacher effectiveness and student rated teacher effectiveness, Emotional intelligence scale (EIS, 2007), Teacher Effectiveness Scale (TES, 2010) and Teacher Rating Scale (TRS, 2003) were administered. The examination discover a huge connection amongst EI and teacher effectiveness, while gender scores were discovered autonomous of EI. Kumar (2012), selected 120 secondary school teachers from 12 schools of Rampur District (UP) as a sample of the investigation. To quantify EI, Emotional Intelligence Scale (EIS) was used while a researcher-made scale for professional development and improvement was utilized to gather the required information from teachers' sample. Aftereffects of the investigation indicated a noteworthy and positive connection between EI and the professional advancement of teachers at secondary school.

Tajudin et al., (2014) investigated an impact of emotional intelligence (EI) and job stress (JS) on teaching effectiveness (TE) among Malaysian teachers. An absolute sample of 293 instructors was selected from Malaysian colleges. The discoveries of the investigation found a connection between teachers EI, JS and TE. Teachers with low EI were found to have low TE and increased job performance.

Kaur (2014) investigated the connection between teaching competency and the EI of secondary school teachers at Amritsar, India. Sample of the study was 100 secondary school teachers who were being evaluated on General Teaching Competency Scale (GTCS), and Emotional Intelligence Scale (EIS). The consequences of the examination provide a generous and positive connection between teachers' teaching competencies and their EI.

Hassan et al., (2015) investigated the relationship between EI and TE of teachers at University Teknologi MARA (UiTM), Puncak Alam, Selangor. Researcher arbitrarily selected a sample of 155 teachers at UiTM, Puncak Alam, and Selangor. Results indicated a positive and significant connection between EI abilities and teaching effectiveness of university teachers. Results further revealed enhanced teachers commitment towards their job with high level of EI.

It has been suggested that high EI of teachers is reflected in a class room situation in the shape of a healthy and productive relationship with students (Olson, et. al., 1989; Brackett & Katulak, 2006; Brackett, Rivers, & Salovey, 2011) effective classroom management skills (Nelson et al., 2005) effective and productive communication skills, stress and conflict management skills (Brackett & Katulak, 2005) decision making and problem-solving skills (Bar On, 2006; Mayer & Salovey, 1997; Salovey, Mayer & Caruso, 1995;Nelson et al., 2005;) adaptability, flexibility, positive approach and confidence (Bar On, 2006; Nelson et al.,2005) good behaviour, management skills, goal-achieving behavior and sense of pleasure and achievement at the workplace, listening, recognizing and appreciating every learner in the classroom, better dealing with their expectations (Mortiboys, 2013) and source of inspiration, leadership, and dynamism (Brackett & Katulak, 2007).

Only an emotionally healthy teacher is blessed with the ability to create and manipulate an emotionally healthy and safe learning atmosphere secured by trust and self-esteem (Nelson et al., 2005). This kind of atmosphere can inspires positive interaction with students and colleagues, and also inspire students for willing participation and academic excellence (Bracket & Katlak, 2007; Fer, 2004; Mayer, Salovey & Caruso, 2004; Nelson et al., 2005). In short, the findings of such studies highlighted that teachers' EI skills have a strong linkage with their TE.

2.6   Literature on Emotional Intelligence in Pakistan

Shahzad (2012) carried out a study "Impact of Emotional Intelligence on university teachers' performance" in Punjab University Lahore. She conveniently selected 170 university teachers as a sample of the study. Bar-On EQ-i: Short along with the teaching effectiveness scale was used for collecting data. Researcher found university teachers in Punjab with low and underdeveloped socio-emotional intelligence; she also found a significant relationship between teacher's EI and TE in the classroom.

Mahmud (2013) conducted a study to find out the impact of EI on the performance of university teachers at Punjab University, Pakistan tried to define the parameters of teacher performance and various dimensions of EI. Two universities were conveniently selected by the researcher, while the sample comprised of 100 teachers from universities. Results of the study revealed a positive relationship between teachers' EI and their performance at work place.

Bibi et al., (2015) tried in their study to explore the relationship between EI of university teachers and their Coping strategies in Khyber Pakhtunkhwa. Researcher adopted a convenient sampling technique, and conveniently selected a sample of 222 male and 152 female teachers. To collect data regarding EI of teachers Self-Report Measure of Emotional Intelligence and Brief Cope Scale (in Urdu) was used to collect data regarding their coping strategies. Statistical analysis of the study found a significant relationship between EI and coping strategies of teachers.

Mohamad & Jais (2016) carried out a study "emotional intelligence and job performance: a study among Malaysian teachers" to examine the role of EI of teachers in relation to their' job performance. Researchers selected 212 teachers from 6 secondary schools as a sample of the study. Findings of the study revealed a substantial relationship between teachers' EI and job performance at work place.

Naqvi et al., (2016) led a study on the topic of the relationship between EI and performance of the secondary school teachers at secondary level in Lahore, Pakistan. Researchers selected 950 teachers from secondary schools comprising both genders. They adopted a Trait Emotional Intelligence Questionnaire Short Form (TEIQue-SF) from K.V Patride to assess the level of their EI. While teachers' performance was assessed through SSC annual examination results of class 10 led by Board of intermediate and secondary Education (BISE), Lahore. Results of the study revealed a significant relationship between teachers' EI and their performance.

Haq (2017) in his research investigated an effect of EI on teacher's job performance in the higher education institutions of Punjab, Pakistan. The researcher inferred a sample size of 166 university teachers from Punjab. Key discoveries uncovered a noteworthy effect of EI over teachers' job performance.

Hassan (2018) conducted a study to inspect a connection between EI and job performance of teachers in higher education institutions of Pakistan. 166 teachers from colleges of Central Punjab were selected as the sample of the investigation. Results of the study indicates that there is a critical effect of EI on teacher's performance.

Latif (2018) investigated EI as a better indicator of the successful job performance of female teachers at secondary schools in Pakistan. He additionally uncovered a reality that EI has a critical association with job fulfillment. 210 female teachers were arbitrarily selected as a sample of the examination. Four instruments, Emotional Intelligence Test (Schutte et al., 1998) Job Satisfaction Scale (Warr, Cook & Wall, 1979) Organizational Commitment Questionnaire (Mowday, Steers & Porter, 1979) and Continuance Commitment Subscale (Allen &Meyer, 1990) were utilized to gauge the factors under investigation. Discoveries of the investigation uncovered that teachers with better Ei aptitudes have more job fulfillment and their students likewise indicated enhanced scholastic presentation. Other than this Many Pakistani researchers have contemplated the factors that straightforwardly or in a roundabout way constitutes EI. Teachers' EI is neglected and not a much-inquired factor in Pakistan. Some work has been conducted on EI, teachers' emotional intelligence and their teaching effectiveness (Shehzad, 2012) the effect of EI on the performance of university teachers (Mahmud, 2013). Numerous researchers have considered different factors that can constitute EI, for example, teachers' emotional intelligence and adapting strategies among university teachers (Bibi et al., 2015) teachers' interpersonal relationship (Bhatti, 2009) conflict resolution approaches in schools (Basit et al., 2010; Siraj ud Din et al., 2011) emotional intelligence and workers' performance (Chaudhry&Usman,2011) job fulfillment and commitment of teachers

(Chughtai & Zafar, 2006; Malik et al., 2010) helpful relationship and professional responsibility of teachers (Shah, 2012) effect of non-verbal correspondence on teaching and students performance (Butt, 2011) students management skills of teachers (Baig, 2011) and professional pride and self-esteem of teachers (Mushtaq, et. al., 2012; Tabassum et al., 2012).

The emotional competency of a teacher is important for an effective teaching-learning process and for socio-emotional development of learners (Ramana, 2003). High EI of teachers leads to high job satisfaction and professional success (Hassan et al., 2015). Emotional intelligence and organizational commitment of college teachers (Shafiq, & Rana, 2016) emotional intelligence and its impact on academic performance of students (Malik, 2016) the relationship between self-esteem and emotional intelligence among university students (Bibi et al., 2016).

CHAPTER-3

METHOD AND PROCEDURE

The chapter comprises detail of the research design used, population and sample distribution, instruments that were being used to collect data, and thorough and comprehensive analysis of the data being collected from the study. The study is constructed on the collection and analysis of quantitative data to examine and discuss the association and bond between two variables i.e. EI and TE.

3.1 Research Design

The research configuration selected for the research study is correlational research as the reason for the study is to discover the connection between teachers' emotional intelligence and their teaching effectiveness.

3.2 Research Population

Participants for this research are comprised of teachers and students of higher secondary schools in Khyber Pakhtunkhwa. According to the information derived from the Annual Statistical Report of the Educational Management Information System (EMIS, 2015-16), there were 464 higher secondary schools in Khyber Pakhtunkhwa. Among these, 305 schools were for boys and 159 for girls. There were total of 269440 students in the higher secondary schools of KP, 168709 were male students while 100731 were female students. Out of the total 10,996 teachers working in these schools, 7635 were male teachers while 3361 were female teachers.

3.3 Sample Size and its Distribution

Quantitative researches generally don't have to gather information from the entire population, if the number of sample of interest is huge or scattered topographically cluster sampling is the best possible technique of obtaining a representative sample. (Gay, L. R. et al., 2012). Out of twenty-five (25) districts of KP, utilizing cluster sampling technique, study was conducted in seven (07) districts of KP i.e. Peshawar, Kohat, Lakki Marwat, Mansehra, Mardan, Malakand, and Swat.

According to Krejcie and Morgan table (1970), if the population size is between 4500-5000, a sample size of three hundred and fifty-seven (357) is enough to represent the whole population. The total sample of the research study from selected districts was three hundred and fifty-seven (357). To guarantee desired representation of relevant sub-groups i.e. male and female stratified sampling was used. It is the process of selecting a sample that represent the sub-groups of population in the same proportion in which they exist in the population (Gay, L. R. et al., 2012). Using stratified proportional sampling, two hundred and forty-three (243) male teachers from Government Higher Secondary Schools for boys and one hundred and fourteen (114) female teachers from Government Girls Higher Secondary Schools were selected. From each district number of schools were proportionally selected for research purpose. A total sample of six (06) teachers (three science teachers i.e. biology, physics and chemistry; three humanities teachers i.e. Islamic history and Urdu literature and civics, and thirty (30) students were selected from each school. The total size of the sample was thirty-six (36) respondents from each school.

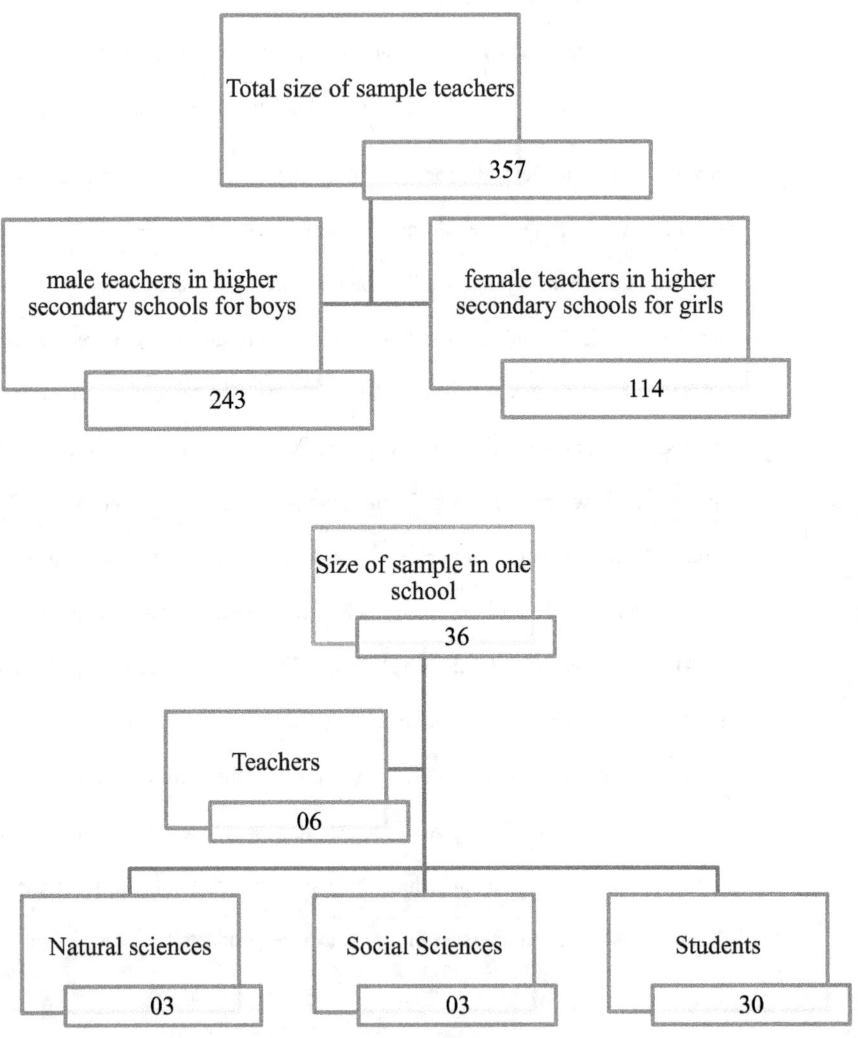

Figure 3.1 Graphic Description of the Sample

3.4 Demographic Characteristics of Teacher Respondents

In the data collection phase along with two research instruments i.e. Self-Report Measure of Emotional Intelligence (SRMEI) and Teaching Effectiveness Scale (TES), an additional sheet was attached with a questionnaire to collect information about the demographic characteristics of respondents.

Table 3.1 Demographic profile of teacher respondents

Variable	Description	Percentage
Qualification	MA/M.Sc.	78%
	M.Phil./Ph.D.	22%
Gender	Male	69%
	Female	31%
Age	25-35	35%
	36-45	45%
	46+	20%
Marital status	Single	44%
	Married	56%

Interpretation

3.1.1 Teachers' Age and Gender

About 69% of teachers in the study were male and 31% are female. The age of participants ranges from 21 to above 51.about 35% of teachers were of 25-35 years, 45% were in 36-45 while 20% were in the age range of 45+ years.

3.1.2 Teachers' Marital Status

About 44% of teachers involved in the research process are single while 56% of teachers were married.

3.1.3   Teacher's Qualification

The majority of the research participants involved are MA/MSC qualified, their proportion was 78% while a little sample of the study was M.Phil. /Ph.D. i.e. 22%.

3.5   Instrumentation

Keeping in view the nature of the study, the researcher decided to use the following instruments to assess teacher's EI and their effectiveness at the workplace.

3.5.1   Background Variables Questionnaire

To collect data or investigate some personal information from the participants of the study, the researcher developed a questionnaire about teachers' demographic characteristics such as rank, gender, marital status, age, and qualification and teaching disciplines. This additional sheet was attached to an instrument used to investigate the EI of teachers.

3.5.2   Self-Report Measure of Emotional Intelligence (2010)

The researcher adopted a scale called the Self-Report Measure of Emotional Intelligence (2010) for the said research purpose to find out teachers EI. This research meant to collect information from prospective group of teachers using the Self-Report Measure of Emotional Intelligence (2010). The SRMEI (2010) is an instrument used to measure Emotional Intelligence, published by the National Institute of Psychology, Quaid e Azam University Islamabad. It was developed keeping in view the culture of the social and emotional setting of Pakistani culture. The reliability and validity of the instrument are well established in the Pakistani context. This test was used to determine the EI of teachers with legal permission of the authority. SRMEI (2010), contains 60 items and employs a 5 point response scale ranging from 'always to never'. The 5-point Likert instrument is rated with 5 for 'always', 4 for 'often', 3 for 'sometimes', 2 for 'rarely' and 1 for 'never'. The test contains 27 positively phrased items while 33 negatively phrased items that require reversed scoring. The highest score range for SRMEI is 300 while the lowest is 60. Scoring was done on 3 composite scales that comprises scores on facets; the three facets of the scale are emotional self-regulation, emotional self-awareness, and interpersonal skills. While the sub scales of emotional self-regulation include adaptability, emotional reactivity management, emotional stability, conscientiousness, and achievement drive. Sub-scales of emotional self-awareness involves self-awareness, perceived assessment and self-confidence. The interpersonal skills involve empathy, sociability and communication. The test is of normal length and less time-consuming. Test can be completed within 15-20 minutes.

Detail of facets, its scope, serial number in scale and the total number of items in each facet of the SRMEI is given below;

Table 3.2 Explanation of Subscales, its Scope, and Number of Items (SRMEI)

self-report Measure of Emotional Intelligence (2010)

Sub-scale	Scope	Serial numbers in the scale	Total Number of items
Emotional Self-Regulation Scale (ESRS)	Adaptability, emotional reactivity management, emotional stability, conscientiousness, achievement drive	1,2,3,4,5,12,13,14,15,16,23,24, 25,26,27,34,35,36,37,44,45,46, 49,50,51,54,57	27
Emotional self-awareness scale (ESAS)	Self-awareness, perceived self-assessment, confidence	6,7,8,17,18,19,28,29,30,38,39,4 0,47,48,52,53,55,56,58,59,60	21
Interpersonal scale(ISS)	Empathy, sociability, communication	9,10,11,20,21,22,31,32,33,41,4 2,43	12

Source. Source: Self-report Measure of Emotional Intelligence (SRMEI) (2010). Technical Manual. Islamabad Pakistan: National Institute of Psychology.

Table 3.2 is a detailed description of the SRMEI scale. The scale is comprised of three sub-scales including emotional Self-Regulation Scale (ESRS), Emotional Self-Awareness Scale (ESAS) and Interpersonal Scale (ISS). There are total number of twenty-seven (27) items under ESRS including facets of adaptability, emotional reactivity management, emotional stability, conscientiousness and achievement drive. Sub-scale of ESAS is comprised of twenty-one statements covering facets of self-awareness, perceived self-assessment, and self-confidence. The last sub-scale is called ISS, which involves twelve (12) statements covering facets of empathy, sociability and communication.

Table 3.3 Positive and Negative Statements in SRMEI (scale-wise)

Sub-scales of SRMEI	The Serial number of Positively phrased statements	The Serial number of Negatively phrased items
Emotional Self-Regulation scale (ESRS) (total=27)	4,15,26	1,2,3,5,12,13,14,16,23,24,25, 27,34,35,36, 37,44,45,46,49,50,51,54,57
Emotional Self-Awareness scale (ESAS) (total=21)	7,8,18,19,29,30,38,39,40,48,5 3,56,59	6,17,28,47,52,55,58,60
Interpersonal skills scale (ISS) (total=12)	9,10,11,20,21,22,31,32,33,42, 43	41

Source: The SRMEI (self-report measure of emotional intelligence 2010)

Table no 3.3 shows a detail description of positively phrased and negatively phrased items in all the three sub-scales of SRMEI. Sub-scale of ESRS includes three (03) positively phrased statements while twenty-four (24) negatively phrased statements. Another sub-scale of SRMEI i.e. ESAS involves thirteen (13) positively phrased and eight (08) negatively phrased items. ISS which is the last sub-scale of SRMEI is comprised of eleven (11) positively phrased and one (01) negatively phrased statement.

Table 3.4 Positive and Negative statements in SRMEI (facet wise)

Facets	Total items	Positively phrased statements	Negatively phrased statements
Adaptability	8	-	1,12,23,34,44,49,54,57
Emotional reactivity management	6	-	2,13,24,35,45,50
Emotional stability	6	-	3,14,25,36,46,51
Conscientiousness	3	4,15,26	-
Achievement drive	4	-	5,16,27,37
Self-awareness	9	38,59	6,17,28,47,52,55,58
Perceived self-assessment	8	7,18,29,39,48,53,56	60
Self-confidence	4	8,19,30,40	-
Empathy	4	9,20,31	41
Sociability	4	10,21,32,42	-
Communication	4	11,22,33,43	-

Source: SRMEI (self-report measure of emotional intelligence 2010)

Table no 3.4 is the detailed description of positively phrased and negatively phrased items in all the eleven (11) facets of the three subscales of SRMEI. Three (03) of the facets of SRMEI don't have any positive statements i.e. facets of adaptability, emotional reactivity management and emotional stability. While four (04) of the facets don't involve any negatively phrased statements i.e. the facet of conscientiousness, self-confidence, sociability, and communication.

Table 3.5 Cronbach's Alpha Co-Efficient for SRMEI and its subscale

Measure	No of items	Alpha coefficient
Emotional Self-Regulation Scale (ESRS)	27	.82
Emotional Self-Awareness Scale (ESAS)	21	.83
Interpersonal Skills Scale (ISS)	12	.67
SRMEI (total)	60	.91

Source: SRMEI (self-report measure of emotional intelligence 2010)

Table 3.5 shows the high reliability of SRMEI i.e. a=.91 which is quite satisfactory. It shows a high alpha coefficient for all subscales of SRMEI i.e. for ESAS a=.83, ESRS=.82, ISS=.67

Table 3.6 Cronbach's Alpha Coefficient for SRMEI and its subscale

Measures	ESRS	ESAS	ISS	Total
Emotional Self-Regulation Scale (ESRS)	-	.82**	.38**	.94**
Emotional Self-Awareness Scale (ESAS)	-	-	.34**	.92**
Interpersonal Skills Scale (ISS)	-	-	-	.55**

Source: The SRMEI (Self-Report Measure of Emotional Intelligence 2010)

Table 3.6 shows that all the sub-scales of SRMEI are significantly correlated and linked with each other.

3.6   Description of Subscales and Facets of SRMEI

3.6.1   Emotional Self-Regulation Scale (ESRS)

This subscale of SRMEI includes 27 items, having facets of adaptability, emotional reactivity management, emotional stability, conscientiousness and achievement drive. Scores on this scale range from 27 to 135. It is composed of 24 negatively phrased and 3 positively phrased statements. A person high on this scale is considered as an emotionally self-regulated person, who can effectively deal with unpleasant and challenging situations. A person who is having the flexibility to adapt to new and demanding situations. They are ready to assimilate and accommodate their behavior according to the demands of the situations. They are self-disciplined people who can productively express their emotions. They have a strong urge to achieve goals and set future targets. They can better control their anger without losing their temper. A high score on this scale is an indication of high emotional self-regulation while low scores indicate the absence of these skills. The scale further contains five facets including adaptability, emotional reactivity management, emotional stability, conscientiousness and achievement drive.

3.6.2   Emotional Self-Awareness Scales (ESAS)

This subscale consists of 21 items composed of self-awareness, perceived self-assessment, and self-confidence. Scores on this scale range from 21 to 105. It comprised of 8 negatively and 13 positively phrased items. A high score on this subscale specifies that an individual can understand his feelings, also know how these feelings can influence their personal and social life. Emotionally self-aware people know their strengths and weaknesses. They also believe in their strengths and can use their strengths positively and productively way, and also know how to overcome their weaknesses. Facets of this sub- scale of SRMEI include self-awareness, perceived self-awareness, and self-confidence.

3.6.3 Interpersonal Skills Scale (ISS)

This 12 item subscale represents the social skills of an individual. This subscale is composed of the facets of empathy, sociability and communication. The score range for this subscale is 12 to 60. It is comprised of 1 negatively and 11 positively phrased statements. People high in interpersonal skills indicate that they have good communication skills; they can positively convey their message. It also shows that these people can maintain good and healthy relationships. They are friendly, warm and empathetic. They are always available and approachable to help people. This sub-scale also contains three facets namely empathy, sociability, and communication.

Self-Report Measure of EI is developed to work in Pakistani context and culture. The scale is inspired by Goleman's (2001) model of EI. SRMEI is a reliable and valid instrument to evaluate EI. SRMEI measures three dimensions of EI which includes emotional self-awareness, interpersonal skills, and emotional self-regulation.

3.6.4 Administering and Scoring Guidelines for using SRMEI (2010)

Scoring was done after the data entry process in SPSS 20 version. Respondents took 15-20 minutes to complete the scale. The score range for SRMEI is from 60-300. High scores on SRMEI reflect better emotional stability of a respondent. Sum of the raw scores of respondents were converted into the mean of the total score. A brief interpretative guideline of SRMEI is provided to calculate the scores and evaluate the social and EI of teachers. The raw score for every item on a report can ranges between 1-5.

Table 3.7 Describes the Scale for Positive Statements of a Self-Report Measure of Emotional Intelligence

1	Never
2.	Rarely
3.	Sometimes
4.	Often
5.	Always

Source. SRMEI (Self-Report Measures of Emotional intelligence, 2010)

Table 3.7 indicated the scale for positive of SRMEI such as the 5 point scale is rated as 5 for 'always', 4 for 'often', 3 for 'moderate', 2 for 'rarely', and 1 for 'never'.

Table 3.8 Description of Scale for Negative Statements of Self-Report Measure of Emotional Intelligence

1	Always
2.	Often
3.	Sometimes
4.	Rarely
5.	Never

Source. SRMEI (Self-Report Measure of Emotional Intelligence, 2010)

Table 3.8 represents the scale for negative SRMEI items i.e. which need to be coded in a reversed manner, i.e. 1=always, 2=often, 3=sometimes, 4=often, 5=never.

3.6.5   Guideline for Scoring Overall SRMEI

The submission of raw score on total items of a test provides an individuals' accumulative score of EI. Scores on SRMEI can ranges from 60-300. Possible score on the Sub-scale of SRMEI i.e. ESRS ranges from 27-135, scores on ESAS ranges from 21-105, while potential scores on RMS range from 12-60.

Table 3.9 Potential Range of scores on overall SRMEI (2010)

Range	Guideline
228 and above	Enriched emotional and social skills
151-227	Satisfactory skills
150 and below	Area for improvement (low socio-emotional skills

Table 3.9 shows possible and definite score ranges on every facet with overall SRMEI. The higher the SRMEI score the better and enhanced emotionally skilled a person will be. Potential range and interpretation guideline are different for all the sub-scales of a scale, as the number of items on all sub scales is different. A teacher who scored 150 or below 150 lies in the category of low socio-emotional skills. Teachers who secure a score of 151-227 lies in the category with satisfactory EI skills with room for improvement. While teachers with high socio-emotional skills score 228 and above on the SRMEI scale.

Table 3.10 Potential Range of Scores on Sub-Scales of SRMEI (2010)

Scales	No. of items	Potential range	Interpretation Guideline		
			Need improvement	Satisfactory	Effective
ESRS	27	27-135	27-68	69-102	103-135
ESAS	21	21-105	21-52	53-78	79-105
ISS	12	12-60	12-30	31-45	46-60

Source: ESRS (Emotional Self-Regulation skills), ESAS (Emotional Self-Awareness skills), ISS (Inter-Personal skills)

Table 3.10 describes and presents interpretation guidelines of SRMEI scores under three category i.e. teachers with EI low skills who needs improvement, teachers with satisfactory EI skills and teachers with high and effective skills.

3.7   Teaching Effectiveness Scale (TES)

The purpose of the research was to examine the impact of EI of teachers on their TE. To measure TE, researcher designed a Teaching Effectiveness Scale with the help of already available scales and experts in the field. The researcher developed "teaching effectiveness scale" contains an area of teaching which is directly or indirectly associated with EI or which could be the obvious traits of a teachers as a result of EI like empathy, having good and healthy interpersonal relationships and positive communication. Subscales of Teaching Effectiveness Scale (TES) designed by the researcher involves (a) Teaching and Pedagogical Skills (TPS), (b) Classroom Management skills (CMS), (c) Relationship Management Skills (RMS).

3.7.1   Generation of Item Pool

The researcher extracted a total number of 50 statements form informal discussions with students, informal interviews with teachers, and from the available teacher rating scale developed nationally and internationally, also from the literature review on effective and emotionally intelligent teachers' characteristics. For this purpose researcher conveniently selected students of the first semester of Bachelor of Science (BS) program of eight departments of the university also had informal settings with students of 2nd year at various government and private colleges to inquire about the traits and characters of teachers they like and dislike. The researcher also went through a detailed literature review of other researchers about teacher characteristics that make them an effective teacher. The researcher also studied on different national and international teachers' effectiveness scale available. So, after detailed discussion and studying literature review, the researcher acquired a list of competencies, which helped the researcher to develop a teacher effectiveness scale for research purposes.

3.7.2 Expert Evaluation of Items

After preparing a list of 50 statements of the item pool for developing the initial format of teaching effectiveness scale, it was being discussed with few experts of the field to seek their opinion for identifying the unclear, inappropriate, and double barrel statements. The experts who were having insight into the research problem were taken as expert judges. 15 experts were being taken from the field of research and teaching at multiple levels. They were enquired for checking of quality, relevance, validity of the sub-themes and items. The researcher with the help of experts tried to make it sure that items included in the scale should be according to the principles of teaching at a higher secondary level relevant with the traits of EI. Experts were requested to increase the excellence and validity of all the facets by modifying the relevant statements and discarding or excluding irrelevant statements for the validity of the instrument. Validity is a degree to which any instrument assesses what it proposed to assess (Carmines & Zeller, 1979). The process of TES development went through a validation process to confirm that questions in an instrument were clear, well defined, easy to understand, and covered topics relevant to TE.

Content validity there are various approaches to ensure the content validity of test items. Researcher in this study used empirical techniques to calculate the content validity (CVI) and the content validity ratio proportion (CVR), (Armstrong et al., 2005 and Zamzadev et.al., 2015).

1.　CVI: It is the most extensively utilized technique to evaluate the content validity of any scale and it can be easily and effectively calculated using the Item-CVI (I-CVI) and the Scale-level-CVI (S-CVI) (Zamzadev et.al, 2015). I-CVI is acquired by processing the complete number of specialists rating of going from calculating the content validity index (CVI) and the content validity ratio (CVR) (Armstrong et al., 2005 & Zamanzadeh et al., 2015). I-CVI is obtained by computing the total number of experts rating of ranging from "very relevant" to "not relevant" for each item, which is then divided by the total number of the professional experts being selected. Where the estimation of I-CVI >0.79 implies the item is applicable and relevant. While values somewhere in the range of 0.70 or less than 0.79 mean the item should be cautiously modified, moreover the item is eliminated if the esteem is underneath 0.70. Likewise, S-CVI is being calculated using the total number of items that have attained a grade or ranking of "very relevant". There are two practices to compute S-CVI, i.e. one method is The Universal Agreement (UA) among experts (S-CVI/ UA), and the other tactic is Average CVI (S-CVI/Ave). S-CVI/UA is calculated by accumulation (adding) of all items with I-CVI equal to 1 and then divided by the total number of items. Whereas S-CVI/Ave is calculated by taking the sum of the I-CVIs and then dividing by the total number of items (Zamanzadehet.al, 2015). S-CVI/UA $\geq$ 0.8 and a S-CVI/Ave $\geq$ 0.9 demonstrates that test items have amazing content validity (Shi et al., 2012).

2.   CVR: Another method of experimental examination is CVR, which inspect how fundamental or significant the test items are (Yamada et.al, 2010). CVR scores range between 1 and$-$1, a high score on CVR reveals a better level of agreement among experts (Zamanzadeh et al., 2015). The formula used to check CVR is CVR $= (N_e - N/2)/ (N/2)$, where N_e is the number of panelists to evaluate the essentiality of test items while N is the whole number of panelists/ experts to check the validity of an instrument (Zamanzadeh et al., 2015).To evaluate the relevancy and essentiality of items in the instrument, the

experts were given an appraisal sheet comprised of four investigations: 1) the relevancy/significance of each test item (how important the question is); 2) the clarity of test items (how clear the wording is); 3) the essentiality test items (how necessary the question is); and 4) endorsements for improvement. To check relevancy, 4-point Likert scale was used and responses include: 1 = not relevant, 2 = somewhat relevant (need some correction), 3=quite relevant and 4 = very relevant. Ratings of 3 and 4 are considered content valid while 1 and 2 are considered content invalid (Wynd et al., 2003). To evaluate clarity of questionnaire 3-point Likert scale was used, 1 = not clear, 2 = item needs some revision; and 3 = very clear, and also for essentiality 3-point Likert item scale was used: 1 = not essential; 2=useful, but not essential; and 3 = essential (Zamanzadeh et al., 2015). An extra sheet was provided for experts recommendations. A minimum number of 5 people is recommended to evaluate the instrument to show their agreement. Content Validity of the instrument developed for this study was determined by 15 experts (n = 15).

After the experts' observation of the scale content validity ratio (CVR) and the content validity index (CVI) was determined. In the phase of CVR assessment, 9 questions obtained a score of less than 0.62 and were omitted. Finally, 41 items were retained with content validity.

Table 3.11 CVI & CVR of Teaching Effectiveness Scale

Sr. #	CVR	Sr. #	CVR
1	0.86	23	1.00
2	0.86	24	1.00
3	1.00	25	1.00
4	0.86	26	0.86
5	0.73	27	1.00
6	1.00	28	1.00
7	0.86	29	0.86
8	1	30	0.73
9	1	31	0.86
10	1	32	0.86
11	1	33	0.86
12	0.86	34	0.86
13	0.86	35	0.73
14	0.86	36	0.86
15	0.86	37	0.86
16	0.73	38	1
17	1	39	1
18	1	40	1
19	0.86	41	1
20	1.00		
21	1.00		
22	1.00	**CVI**	**0.91**

The content validity ratio and cumulative CVI of various items are given in the table 3.11. Forty-one items were declared as relevant items to TE and their I-CVIs ranged from 0.73 to 1.00. Seventeen items had an ICVI = 1, thirteen items had an ICVI= 0.86 and eleven had a score of 0.73.

CVR results

The CVR was generated for each item of teaching effectiveness scale. Twenty (20) items had a CVR of 1.00, seventeen (17) had a CVR of 0.86, four statements scored 0.73, five with a score of 0.33, while four a score of 0.00. The average CVR value found was 0.91. Items scored less than. 60 on CVR were excluded. Clarity Results (individual items and overall questionnaire) was calculated using 6 evaluators on a 3-point Likert Scale i.e. (1 = not clear, 2 = somewhat clear, 3 = very clear).

3.7.3   Description of Sub-Scales of Teaching Effectiveness Scale

To investigate the level of TE researcher developed an instrument, the teaching effectiveness scale for the said research purpose. The researcher tried to establish the reliability and validity of the instrument. TES is of normal length, easy to understand and less time-consuming. Test can be completed within 10-15 minutes.

Table 3.12 Description of Subscales, Their Scope, Number of Items of (TES) Teaching Effectiveness Scale

Sub Factors	Scope	No. of items	Sr. # in the final scale
TPS	Ability to teach clearly and effectively	17	1,3,4,5,6,7,8,10,11,12,13,14,15,18,19,20,33
CMS	Effective classroom management skills using time management and behavior management approaches	12	2,9,16,17,24,25,26,27,28,29,30,14
RMS	Teacher-student bond that leads towards effective students' performance	12	21, 22, 23, 31, 32, 34, 35, 36, 37, 38, 39, 40
TES	Overall Teaching effectiveness comprising availability of teacher, productive teacher-student relationship, enthusiastic and facilitative classroom environment, pedagogical skills and classroom management skills as a product of teachers' emotional intelligence.	41	1-41

Source. Content & pedagogical skills (CPS), Classroom management skills (CM), relationship management skills (RMS) Teaching effectiveness (TE)

Table 3.12 signify Description of Subscales, Scope, number of Items and example Items of (TES) Teaching Effectiveness Scale. The scale contains 41 items and employs a 5 point response scale ranging from always to never. The 5-point scale is rated with 5 for the 'always', 4 for 'often', 3 for 'sometimes', 2 for 'rarely' and 1 for 'never'. The lowest score range for TES is 41 while the highest is 205. Scoring on TES was done on three sub-scales that collectively comprise the overall Teaching Effectiveness Scale. The three sub-scales of TES are, teaching and pedagogical skills, class room management skills, and relationship management skills. All the items on TES are positively phrased.

3.7.4   Correlation among TES Sub-Scales

Table 3.13 Explains correlation among TES Sub Factors as

Correlations		TPS	CMS	RMS
TPS	Pearson Correlation	1	.769[**]	.771[**]
CMS	Pearson Correlation	.769[**]	1	.718[**]
RMS	Pearson Correlation	.771[**]	.718[**]	1

**. Correlation is significant at the 0.01 level (2-tailed).

Source. Teaching and pedagogical skills (TPS), Classroom management skills (CMS), relationship management skills (RMS)

Results on table 3.13 revealed that all the sub-scales of teaching effectiveness scale are significantly correlated with each other.

3.7.5   Reliability of Teaching Effectiveness Scale

The reliability coefficient of the Teaching Effectiveness Scale was established and the total reliability of TES was found as 0.87.

Table 3.14 Reliability analysis of teaching effectiveness scale (TES)

Item-total Statistics	Cronbach's Alpha
Teaching and pedagogical skills (TPS)	.835
Class room management skills (CMS)	.788
Relationship management skills (RMS)	.853

Source. Teaching and pedagogical skills (TPS), Classroom management skills (CMS), relationship management skills (RMS)

Table 3.14 shows high reliability of TES i.e. a=.87 which shows high alpha coefficient for all subscales of teaching effectiveness scale (TES) i.e. for TPS a=.83, CMS=.78 and RMS= .85.

3.7.6   Description of Sub-Scales of TES

3.7.6.1 Teaching and Pedagogical Skills

This subscale of TES includes 17 positively phrased items. Score on this scale range from 17 to 85. A high score on TPS indicates that a teacher can achieve student learning objectives, adopt flexible and effective teaching strategies, motivate and engage students, demonstrates flexibility, establishes clear, challenging and viable goals for students, and help them achieve those goals, while engaging students actively in the class room activities. He has the ability to monitors student progress and provides timely and positive feedback on their progress and achievements. Such a teacher can demonstrate high-quality classroom teaching skills which enable all students to achieve their full potential. He has command over his subject and can convey his message keeping in view the individual differences (intellectual, cultural, religious etc.) in the class room. Such a teacher uses different techniques to keep students engage and motivated i.e. using humor in the class room, display his interest and enthusiasm, and creating connectivity in real life and class room situations. He motivates students to learn and accept new challenges with boldness.

3.7.6.2 Classroom Management Skills

This sub scale of TES contains 12 positively phrased items. Score on this sub-scale range from 12-60. A high score on CMS means that a teacher knows individual differences and child psychology, ultimately show respect towards the uniqueness and diversity of each child - and has knowledge of the needs arises from these diversities; he has an understanding of the significance of students motivation for their academic excellence; knows the principles involves in the promotion of discipline. He can make class room environment comfortable for a smooth running of teaching-learning process.

3.7.6.3 Relationship Management Skills (RMS)

Relationship management skills are comprised of 12 positively phrased items. Scores on RMS range from 12-60. A high score on RMS indicates that a teacher can effectively communicate with learners, develops productive relationships with learners, knows, appreciates and responds to individual differences and diversities accordingly, inspires and promotes positive student behavior, can work effectively with all the stakeholders responsible for the care of students. Teacher high on RMS skills can promote constructive and healthy relationships with students which resulted in their academic excellence. They can evaluate and monitor students' achievement and inform parents about their children's progress. Such kind of teacher has a trait of empathy that can understand student's problems and is always available to support them. Adjust easily to changing needs of the daily lives, and can adapt themselves to fit in the situation at hand or to meet the expectations of others and can stay calm in a stressful situation. Such teachers can think carefully about the possible effects of their words, actions, appearance and behaviors on others and maintains stable performance and have controlled emotions when faced with antagonism, hostility, disagreement, and pressure in stressful conditions.

3.7.7 Administering and Scoring Guideline of TES

TES is a researcher-made instrument to rate the teachers in their TE. It is a student report measure to rate their teachers comprised of 41 items on 5-points Likert type scale.

Table 3.15 Descriptions of TES

Score	Picture
1	Never
2	Rarely
3	Sometimes
4	Often
5	Always

The raw score for every item on a scale can range between 1-5. Possible test score can be given as 1= never, 2=rarely, 3=sometimes, 4=often= 5 =always.

The submission of raw scores on items of a test, provides an individuals' total score. Scores on TES can range from 41-205. Possible scores on Sub scale of TES i.e. TPS range from 17-85, scores on CMS range from 12-60 while potential scores on RMS range from 12-60. Table 4.14 shows the possible and actual range of score on all the facets and overall TES. The higher the TES score of the teacher is, the more effective the teacher is in his teaching profession. Potential range and interpretation guideline are different for all the sub scales of a scale, as the number of items on all sub scales is different.

Table 3.16 Reliability Analysis of TES

Reliability Statistics

Cronbach's Alpha	Cronbach's Alpha Based on Standardized Items	No of Items
.992	.992	3

3.8 Data Collection

The researcher visited every district for collecting data accompanied by a few research assistants (university students) who were trained concerning research tools administration. Data was collected with the prior permission of heads of the higher secondary schools. Verbal consent was taken from all the concerned teachers. SRMEI was distributed among teachers of higher secondary schools. The SRMEI also included a separate sheet of demographic information of teachers which was the requirement of the research, including teacher name, subject, workload, education and experience. Students of the same teachers were given TES to evaluate their teacher's performance. Data was collected from the students of the second year so that they were in a better position to evaluate their teachers' performance. Their consent was also taken into consideration for data collection. The purpose of the research was explained to the participants and confidentiality of the data was being ensured.

3.9   Data Analysis

To analyze and interpret the collected data from teachers and students SPSS-20 software package was used. The mean score of SRMEI for teacher respondents and TES for student respondents was calculated. After a brief discussion with the experts, Independent sample t test, ANOVA and Pearson correlation were applied to analyze the data. Detail of analysis techniques is given below;

Table 3.17 Arrangement of Data Analysis according to Research Objectives

Objectives	Instrument	Probable Analyses
1. To determine the level of emotional intelligence of teachers at the higher secondary schools	Self-Report Measure of Emotional Intelligence (2010)	Converting raw scores into mean scores
2.To identify the effect of some demographic variables on EI scores of teachers at the higher secondary level of KP	Self-Report Measure of Emotional Intelligence (2010)	Independent sample T-test and ANOVA
3. To measure teaching effectiveness of teachers at the higher secondary level of KP	Teaching Effectiveness Scale	Converting students raw score of their teachers effectiveness into mean scores
4. To explore the relationship between teachers' emotional intelligence and their teaching effectiveness at the higher secondary level	1.Self-Report Measure of Emotional Intelligence (2010) 2. Teaching Effectiveness Scale by researcher	Pearson correlation coefficient to establish a bond between two variables i.e. Emotional Intelligence and teaching effectiveness

CHAPTER-4

ANALYSIS AND INTERPRETATION OF DATA

This unit of the research dissertation tries to answers the research hypothesis in a detailed way. Every single research hypothesis is addressed one by one using relevant statistical technique.

4.1 Psychometric Properties of Sub-Scales of SRMEI

The total number of teacher respondents who attempted SRMEI scale was 357. The scale was rated on five-point Likert scale i.e. 1=never, 2= rarely, 3=sometime, 4=often, and 5=always. The total raw scores of each respondent was converted into mean scores.

Table 4.1 Descriptive Statistics

SRMEI	N	Minimum	Maximum	Mean	Std. Deviation
ESRS	357	2.29	3.41	2.6907	.44348
ESAS	357	1.57	3.43	2.3001	.55834
ISS	357	2.08	3.03	2.4046	.39699
Total EI	357	2.33	3.37	2.6845	.44166

Source: ESRS= emotional self-regulation scale, ESAS= emotional self-awareness scale, ISS= interpersonal scale, EI= emotional intelligence

Table 4.1 shows a detailed description of SRMEI i.e. Self-Report Measure of Emotional Intelligence. On sub-scale of ESRS responses varies between minimum 2.29 and maximum 3.41 with mean=2.69. The mean value for ESRS i.e. 2.69 has a standard deviation value of 0.44. Another sub-scale of SRMEI i.e. ESAS responses varies between minimum 1.5 and maximum 3.4 with mean=2.3 (standard deviation= 0.55), while on the last sub-scale of ISS responses vary between 2.08 minimum to 3.0

maximum with mean=2.4 (standard deviation= 0.39). Overall the average responses range between minimum 2.33 to maximum 3.37 with a total mean=2.68. The value of standard deviation for mean value=2.68 is 0.44, enlightening low and underdeveloped socio-emotional ability of respondents (teachers), with room for improvement.

4.2   Correlation of Emotional Self-Regulation Scale (ESRS) and Teaching Effectiveness

Table 4. 2 Correlation of ESRS and TE

	N	ESRS	TES	P-value
ESRS	357	1	.897**	.000**
TES	357	.897**	1	.000**

**. Correlation is significant at the 0.05 level (2-tailed).

Source: ESRS= emotional self-regulation scale, TES=teaching effectiveness scale

Pearson correlation coefficient (2-tailed Test) was applied to find the association between teachers' emotional self-regulation and their TE. Findings are illustrated in table 4.2. Looking at the data, it is concluded that there is a significant correlation (i.e. 0.897) between ESRS and TE. The result is statistically significant at 0.05 (2-tailed) with a correlation value of 0.897. Hence rejecting the null hypothesis that there is no significant relationship between teachers' emotional self-regulation skills and TE. It was further inferred that there is a significant relationship between ESRS and TE.

4.3   Correlation of Emotional Self-Awareness Scale (ESAS) and Teaching Effectiveness

Table 4.3 Correlation of ESAS and TE

	N	ESAS	TES	P-value
ESAS	357	1	.709**	.000**
TES	357	.709**	1	.000**

**. Correlation is significant at the 0.05 level (2-tailed).

Source: ESAS= emotional self-awareness scale, TES=teaching effectiveness scale

Table 4.3 shows, Pearson correlation coefficient (test) was applied to test the relation between teachers' emotional self-awareness (ESAS) with TE. It was found that the significance value should be less than 0.05 to accept the hypothesis. The test result is statistically significant on 0.05 (2-tailed) levels with a correlation of .709. Hence Null Hypothesis i.e. there isn't any significant relationship between teachers' emotional self-regulation skills and TE was rejected in the light of accepting H1-Hypothesis, showing a significant correlation between ESAS and TE.

4.4   Correlation of interpersonal skill scale (ISS) and Teaching Effectiveness

Table 4.4 Correlation of ISS and TE

	N	ISS	TES	P-value
ISS	357	1	.938**	.000**
TES	357	.938**	1	.000**

**. Correlation is significant at the 0.05 level (2-tailed).
Source: ISS= interpersonal skill scale, TES=teaching effectiveness scale

Table 4.4 explicit to find out the statistical association between teachers' emotional self-regulation with the TE. Statistical test of Pearson correlation coefficient was used (2-tailed test) over the data. The result is statistically significant on 0.05 level (2-tailed) with a correlation value of 0.938. The tests result thus proves that teachers' interpersonal skills (ISS) and TE are positively correlated, ultimately rejecting the null hypothesis, stating that: there isn't any significant relationship between ISS and TE.

Table 4.5 Psychometric Properties of TES

TES	N	Minimum	Maximum	Mean	Std. Deviation
TPS	357	2.4500	3.5500	2.8288	.46726
RMS	357	2.4000	3.5600	2.8169	.46028
CMS	357	2.3900	3.5900	2.8270	.46779

Source: TES= teaching effectiveness scale, TPS= teaching and pedagogical skills, CMS= class room management skills, RMS= relationship management sills

Table 4.5 indicates the mean score of respondents on teaching and pedagogical skills (TPS) =2.82, the mean score on Classroom Management Skills (CMS) =2.82, while the mean score on the sub scale of Relationship Management Skills (RMS) =2.81. The mean scores on the overall Teaching Effectiveness Scale is 2.82. Interestingly, all mean values are nearer to each, reflecting the value of 2.8, with slight insignificant variation in mean values, revealing low and underdeveloped teaching competencies, with room for improvement.

4.6   Comparison of Teachers' EI at higher secondary level by Gender

An independent sample T-test was applied to find a relationship between teachers' demographic variable (Gender) and SRMEI skills.

Table 4.6 Gender wise comparison of teachers at higher secondary school

SRMEI Scale	Gender	N	Mean	Std. Deviation	p-value	t-value
ESRS	Male	243	2.647243	.5839144	.000	-7.29
	Female	114	3.105877	.4825335		
ESAS	Male	243	2.817737	.4595778	.000	-5.473
	Female	114	3.108070	.4833161		
ISS	Male	243	2.815802	.4608756	.000	-5.484
	Female	114	3.106754	.4809531		
Total EI	Male	243	2.7603	.46208	.000	-6.517
	Female	114	3.1069	.48218		

Source: ESRS= emotional self-regulation scale, ESAS= emotional self-awareness scale, ISS= interpersonal scale, EI= emotional intelligence

Findings illustrated in Table 4.6, show male teachers' mean score M= 2.76, SD= .462 and that of female teachers M=3.10, SD=.482. Mean responses of male teachers on the facet of ESRS: mean= 2.64, SD= 0.58, while female mean responses on the said facet is m=3.10, SD= 0.482. Average male teacher responses for ESAS show mean=2.81, SD= 0.459, while the mean response of female teachers is m= 3.10, SD= 0.483, and the same goes for sub-scale of ISS i.e. mean=2.81. SD= 0.460 for male responses while mean= 3.10, SD=0.480 for female responses. For the two groups to be treated unequal, the significant (2-tailed) values should be less than 0.05. Hence the data confirms a significant relationship between EI and gender. On all the sub-scales of SRMEI female teachers slightly counter pass their male gender. Hence, the null hypothesis (H_0) of the study was rejected i.e. there isn't any significant relationship between teachers demographic variable (gender) and EI. It was thus concluded that females have higher EI skills as compared to their male counterpart (Overall SRMEI= t (-6.517), p is smaller than 0.05).

4.7　Comparison of Teachers' EI at Higher Secondary Level by Marital Status

An Independent sample T-test was applied to find the relationship between teachers' demographic variable (marital status) and SRMEI skills.

Table 4.7 Comparison of teachers by marital status at higher secondary school

SRMEI Scale	Marital status	N	Mean	Std. Deviation	p-value	t-value
ESRS	Single	158	2.678165	.5573608	.001	-3.327
	Married	199	2.885427	.6054825		
ESAS	Single	158	2.799684	.4502093	.000	-3.914
	Married	199	2.998392	.4962012		
ISS	Single	158	2.797911	.4511698	.000	-3.914
	Married	199	2.996683	.4958006		
Total EI	Single	158	2.7586	.46211	.000	-3.896
	Married	199	2.9602	.50333		

Source: ESRS= emotional self-regulation scale, ESAS= emotional self-awareness scale, ISS= Interpersonal scale, EI= Emotional intelligence

Data in Table 4.7 shows married teachers mean scores are significantly different from single teachers in all the three facets of SRMEI i.e. ESRS, ESAS, ISS. On ESRS, the mean score of single teachers is (M=2.67, SD=0.55) while the mean score of Married teachers' (M=2.88, SD=0.60). Single teachers' mean score on the facet of ESAS is (M=2.79, SD=0 .45), while mean scores of married teachers' is (M= 2.99, SD= 0.49). On the last facet of ISS, single teachers' mean scores are (M=2.75, SD=0.46), while those of married teachers' on the same facet are (M=2.90, SD=0.50). P-value was scrutinized at value, 0.05. The significance (2-tailed) level was found to be less than 0.05 for the two groups to be treated as unequal. Therefore it can be concluded that the two counter groups' i.e. single and married teachers group differ significantly on

ESRS, ESAS, ISS and overall SRMEI skills. Null hypothesis (H_0) was rejected i.e. there isn't any significant relationship between teachers demographic variable (marital status) with EI. Statistics showed that there exist a significant relationship between teachers' demographic variable i.e. marital status and EI (Overall SRMEI= t (-3.896), p is smaller than 0.05).

4.8   Comparison of Teacher's EI at Higher Secondary Level by Qualification

An Independent sample T-test was applied to find the relationship between teachers' demographic variable (Qualification) and SRMEI skills.

Table 4.8 Qualification wise comparison of teachers

SRMEI Scale	Qualification	N	Mean	Std. Deviation	p-value	t-value
ESRS	M.A/ M.Sc.	281	2.73	.601233	.001	-3.397
	M.Phil./Ph.D	76	2.99	.5188354		
ESAS	M.A/ M.Sc.	281	2.88	.4806611	.045	-2.011
	M.Phil./Ph.D	76	3.01	.4970517		
ISS	M.A/ M.Sc.	281	2.88	.4815336	.042	-2.038
	M.Phil./Ph.D	76	3.01	.4944152		
Total EI	M.A/ M.Sc.	281	2.8	.48864	.008	-2.679
	M.Phil./Ph.D	76	3.0	.50106		

Source: ESRS= emotional self-regulation scale, ESAS= emotional self-awareness scale, ISS= interpersonal scale, SRMEI= emotional intelligence

Table 4.8 shows that there exists a significant difference between the SRMEI scores of counter groups. Respondents scores in the sub-scale of ESRS with M.A/ M.Sc. have mean values and standard deviation values as: m=2.73 and SD=0.60, while teachers with M.Phil./Ph.D have M=2.99 and SD=0.51. At sub-scale of ESAS teachers with M.A/ M.Sc. have m=2.88 and SD=3.01, while teachers with M.Phil./Ph.D have M=3.01 and SD=0.49. Teachers in the last sub-scale ISS with

M.A/ M.Sc. have m=2.88 and SD=0.48, while teachers with M.Phil./Ph.D have M=3.01 and SD=0.49. Overall ESRS results show teachers score with M.A/ M.Sc. i.e. m=2.8 and SD=0.48, while teachers with M.Phil./Ph.D have M=3.0 and SD=0.50. The significance of the P-value was checked at 0.05 levels and hence the two groups were treated as unequal. The test found a significant relationship between teachers' demographic variable i.e. qualification and their EI skills, thus rejecting the null hypothesis (H_0) that there isn't a significant relationship between EI and teachers' qualifications. It was thus inferred that SRMEI values of two groups differ according to the qualification level of teachers, hence accepting the fact that there exists a significant relationship between teachers' qualification and EI skills (Overall SRMEI= t (-2.679), p is smaller than 0.05).

4.9   Comparison of Teachers' EI at Higher Secondary Level by Age

ANOVA was used to dig out the differences between the mean EI scores of diverse age groups of teachers. Teachers' EI score mean in various age groups is given in Table 4.9.

Table 4.9 Age-wise comparison of Teachers EI Scores

	SRMEI Scale	Sum of Squares	Df	Mean Square	F	p-value (Sig.)
	Between Groups	1.808	2	.904	2.595	.076
ESRS	Within Groups	123.336	354	.348		
	Total	125.144	356			
	Between Groups	1.165	2	.583	2.489	.084
ESAS	Within Groups	82.885	354	.234		
	Total	84.050	356			
	Between Groups	1.126	2	.563	2.402	.092
ISS	Within Groups	82.984	354	.234		
	Total	84.110	356			
	Between Groups	1.329	2	.665	2.738	.066
Total EI	Within Groups	85.939	354	.243		
	Total	87.268	356			

Source: ESRS= emotional self-regulation scale, ESAS= emotional self-awareness scale, ISS= interpersonal scale, SRMEI= emotional intelligence

To find out whether teachers of various age cadres display the same EI skills or not. ANOVA was used to find out whether EI skills are linked with the age of the teacher. Data table 4.9 shows that all three age groups notably display the same results on all the facets of SRMEI i.e. ESRS, ESAS, ISS. It was observed that the significance (2-tailed) level was greater than 0.05 and hence the group variance was treated as equal. Hence accepting the null hypothesis (H_0), that there isn't any significant relationship between age and EI. Thus it was inferred that EI value does not increase with the growing age of teachers [p=.066 which is greater than 0.05].

4.10   Correlation among Sub Factors of SRMEI and TES

Pearson Correlation Coefficient was applied to examine the relationship or association

between teachers' EI and their TE.

Table 4.10 Correlation among Sub Factors of SRMEI and TES

	RMS	CMS	TPS	TES
ESRS	.934**	.932**	.940**	.897**
ESAS	.800**	.820**	.825**	.709**
ISS	.966**	.980**	.986**	.938**
SRMEI	.960**	.973**	.980**	.948**

**. Correlation is significant at the 0.01 level (2-tailed).
Source: ESRS= emotional self-regulation scale, ESAS= emotional self-awareness scale, ISS= interpersonal scale, SRMEI= self-report measure of emotional intelligence, TPS= teaching and pedagogical skills, CMS= class room management skills, RMS= relationship management sills, TES= teaching effectiveness scale

Table 4.10 show that there is a significant relationship between teachers' scores on all

the facets of SRMEI and facets of TES. Which is statistically significant on 0.01

levels (2-tailed Pearson Correlation test) at 0.05 level (2-tailed). It can be concluded

that all the facets of SRMEI and TES are positively correlated, hence accepting the

H1 hypothesis, while rejecting the null hypothesis (H$_0$) of the study i.e. there is no

significant relationship between Emotional Intelligence of teachers and their TE. The

test showed a significant relationship between teachers' EI and TE in the current

study.

CHAPTER-5

CONCLUSION, DISCUSSION AND RECOMMENDATIONS

This chapter of the thesis aims to restate the research objectives, research hypotheses and research method to highlight the findings of the study and to make future recommendations.

Below are the results of the study which highlights its outcomes. The discussion incorporates the prominence of the findings for each research speculation, and includes support from discoveries of other comparative research discoveries. This study investigated the connection between teachers' EI and TE. It was hypothesized that there would not be any positive connection between teachers' EI and their TE and that some demographic variables like age, sex, marital status and qualification do not have any effect on EI of teachers. Significant discoveries of this study are portrayed underneath;

5.1   Findings

On the premise of information investigated, the following were the fundamental discoveries drawn from the study;

1.   The findings of the study revealed that Emotional Self-Regulation has a great influence on the TE of the teachers at the higher secondary level of KP with a correlation of .897.

2.   The study revealed that Emotional Self-Awareness has a significant impact on TE of the teachers at the higher secondary level of KP with a correlation of .709.

3. It has been found that Interpersonal Skills and TE are closely related to each other with a correlation value of .938.

4. Gender wise analysis of the study found female teachers with slightly better EI skills than their male counterparts with an average mean of 3.10.

5. Married teachers were slightly found better than single teachers on all the sub scales of SRMEI with an average mean of 2.96.

6. It has been analyzed through the result of the study that the qualification of the respondents has an impact on the EI of teachers. Teachers with higher qualifications were found better than teachers with masters degrees with an average mean of 3.0.

7. The proposed study revealed the fact that teachers' EI is not linked with age. Teachers of all the age groups were found to display same level of EI.

8. Results of the study concluded that teachers performance at the higher secondary level of KP is with an average mean of 2.82 is not satisfactory and there is dire need to enhance their TE.

9. Statistical analysis of the study led us to the conclusion that all three facets of SRMEI i.e. ESRS, ESAS and ISS are notably linked with all the three sub scales of TE i.e. TPS, CMS and RMS. The overall result is statistically significant on 0.01 levels (2-tailed).

5.2 Conclusion

In light of the findings based on data analysis, the following conclusions were drawn from the study.

It is obvious from the results of the study that teachers at higher secondary level in Khyber Pakhtunkhwa lies at the very threshold of effective functioning. Teachers at higher secondary schools in KP fall roughly at the bottom level of effective functioning, which is an alarming situation. The study revealed an immature and unfledged socio-emotional capacity of teachers, with room for improvement in all the facets of EI skills ultimately affecting their TE. Results of the study, encompassing teachers' EI skills are not satisfactory as they were failed to surpass the average level of EI, so they failed to attain the criteria fundamental to attain a high level of EI. The results of the study can be concluded in a way that teachers at higher secondary schools were unable to deal with their emotions and those of others in an effective way. They were also found with very little urge to improve themselves to meet the new standards of teaching, and were found happy and satisfied with their obsolete methods. The study found them to be more confident in their skin and rigid to adapt a change with the little mental horizon. The study revealed the fact that teachers at the higher secondary level have little knowledge of their strengths and weaknesses and revealed little desire for improvement as they were found satisfied with their existing state. Result also revealed lack of social warmth and difficulty in expressing their emotions. All these factors collectively indicate poor or low EI skills of teachers at higher secondary schools resulting in their low TE.

Students rated their teachers on different facets of the Teaching Effectiveness Scale around or below average. One of the most astonishing and shocking revelation of the study was that not even on single facets of teaching effectiveness scale i.e. Teacher-Student Relationship, Classroom Management, Content and Pedagogy Skills, teachers could reach or surpass the level of effectiveness.

The results of the study led us to the conclusion that female teachers have slightly improved skills and show somehow good results on all the components of ESRS, ESAS and ISS as compare to their counterpart gender. Hence it can be concluded that as far as teachers' EI is concerned, gender is a basis of variation.

The study found married teachers more adaptive, confident, empathetic and helpful towards their students which ultimately resulted in enhanced and healthy relationships with their students and colleagues. It can be concluded that married teachers were found better on all the sub-scales of ESRS, ESAS, ISS and overall SRMEI as compare to teachers respondents who were not married.

The results of the study reveal that qualification also has an impact on enriched socio-emotional intelligence of teachers. Teachers with higher education i.e. M.Phil. And Ph.D. were found to be better than teachers with simple graduation.

Teachers belong to different age groups showed almost the same results on all the three sub-scales i.e. ESRS, ESAS and ISS of EI. It can be concluded that age doesn't have any impact on TE.

The Study revealed a significant relationship between all the facets of EI with all the facets of TE. The relationship between the two variables is statistically significant at the 0.05 level (2-tailed). All the facets of teachers' EI i.e. Emotional Self-Awareness, Emotional Self-Management and Interpersonal Relations and overall EI were found to have a positive correlation with all the three facets of TE i.e. Teacher-Student Relationship, Classroom Management, Content and Pedagogical skill and overall TE. In conclusion, the results of the study were found consistent with the researcher's expectation that teachers' EI is positively correlated with TE. EI is a significant predictor of TE at the higher secondary level. As EI of the teacher is associated with the increased students' academic excellence, enhanced confidence, better communication and management skills, enhancing or enriching teachers' EI may lead towards better students' learning outcomes and success.

5.3   Discussion

Today's nation is on the onset of facing new challenges and demands of the 21st century and to meet these challenges successfully, education is considered as one of the most effective and operative instruments. While to run this education industry effectively in this era of competition and uncertainty, the teacher is regarded as the main pillar of this system. The teacher acts as a builder of the nation to prosper and move forward with rapid growth and progress. Teachers' role is not restricted only to the delivery of knowledge but has a key role in inspiring and molding the mind and personality of students keeping in view the educational reforms and challenges. The teacher has so many roles to perform at the same time, sometimes he is required to play the role of facilitator, sometimes a guide, a counselor, a friend and so on. The teacher also has to face challenges related with educational reforms, including day by day changing technology, newly introduced teaching strategies and techniques, students' academic performance, heavy work load, parental and societal demands and expectations, declining learning interests of students, increased stress, frustration, aggression, and violence among students etc. All these demands and work pressure can put the teacher under stress and emotional challenges. So there is dire need to enhance teacher's EI to increase their effectiveness.

As mentioned in the previous chapter, teachers at the higher secondary level in Khyber Pakhtunkhwa fall at the bottom of effective functioning, while a major part of the cadre didn't even surpass the average capacity of EI skills. In the current study TE as a core result of their EI skills is evaluated on three parameters i.e. teaching and pedagogical skills, classroom management skills and Relationship management skills. In the present study all the facets that come under the category of teachers' EI are found in association with all the described facets of TE.

The present research study found a significant relationship between EI and the teacher-student relationships. This phenomenon is further supported by other studies in the field (Brackett & Katlak, 2006; Fer, 2004; Brackett, Rivers, & Salovey, 2011; Kremenitzer & Miller, 2008; Nelson et al., 2005; Wilson et al., 2009). According to Lopes, Salovey, Cote and Beers (2005) EI skills are associated with the value of individuals' social interactions. Students only come to the teachers whom they believe and can trust. Such kind of connection creates an emotional attachment between the two stake holders. Salami (2007) is also of the view that an emotionally intelligent teacher promotes students' learning thirst and show respect towards their emotions. This connection subsequently, results in a healthy teacher-student relationship. It is discovered in several other studies that EI has a prominent role to play in developing healthy, interactive and productive relationship between teacher and student (Bracket & Katlak, 2006; Fer, 2004; Brackett, Rivers & Salovey, 2011; Kremnitzer & Miller, 2008; Nelson et al., 2005; Wilson et al., 2009). To motivate students and to encourage them to achieve the best in their life teachers also need to develop an emotional attachment with them (Labaree, 2000). Raider-Roth (2005) claimed that a trustworthy and effective teacher-student relationship is crucial in enhancing students' capacity to learn. Salami (2007) stated that healthy teacher-student relationship is the result of teacher EI. A lot of other studies by different researchers established a positive relationship between teacher EI and healthy relationships with students, colleagues and friends. (Brackett & Katulak, 2006; Cohen & Sandy, 2007; Wols, Scholte, & Qualter, 2015, Jennings & Greenberg, 2009).

Teachers' EI was also found to be connected with effective Classroom Management, which is further supported by studies of other researchers (Chechi, 2012; Kremnitzer & Miller, 2008; Nelson et al., 2005) who also found a significant relationship between the two variables i.e. EI skills and class room management. Jeloudar et al., (2011), suggested that teachers' EI has resulted in a disciplined classroom environment. Salami (2007) emphasized that an emotionally intelligent teacher engages students in multiple classroom activities to reduce discipline hurdles. An emotionally intelligent teacher knows well how to deal with disruptive behaviors. They set clear and achievable goals to maximize student's participation and minimize disciplinary problems in the classroom. Classroom management is described as teachers' activities which aim at creating a conducive environment to enhance students' socio-emotional health and academic success (Pianta, 2006). McCarthy et al., (2015), also concluded that teachers with better understanding and knowledge of emotional management have an increased capability of class room management and can better deal with student's behavioural problems.

An emotionally intelligent teacher is capable to create an environment that is emotionally safe with space for trust and self-esteem (Nelson et al., 2005) better able to encourage positive social interaction, and enhanced academic excellence among students (Brackett & Katlak, 2007; Fer, 2004; Nelson et al., 2005). One of the very prominent and major reasons for student's habit of not attending the classes regularly is teachers' attitude. On the contrary, students rush to those classes only where they find an emotionally safe environment, where they are encouraged to achieve their goals, where they do not have to pass through competitive and stressed circumstances, where their accomplishments are being appreciated, where they can easily take a risk and give green signals to challenges without fear of penalty and failure, where they always find something valuable and interesting to do; where they are treated as being unique from another student, and where their uniqueness is being valued. An emotionally intelligent teacher exhibits patience in all sorts of learning environment, believe in students' strengths, and encourage them to achieve their best (Salami, 2007). Oliver and Reschly, (2010) and Oliver et al., (2011) also emphasized the importance of teacher's EI and behaviour management skills of teachers for better student's academic outcomes.

The study found a strong link between EI skills and Content and pedagogical skills of a teacher. Ghanizadeh and Moafian (2010) also in their study found a notable relationship between teachers' EI with content and pedagogical skills. The teacher's knowledge of his subject, performance, and behavior display during teaching-learning process is defined as the teaching style of a teacher. Applying a suitable teaching style and teaching technique has a prominent effect on learners' performance. Best teaching technique can be defined as adopting methodology to enhance student's understanding and motivating and inspiring them to think judgementally, be creative and making them confident and faith in their abilities (Iurea, Neacsu, Safta, & Suditu, 2011). Salami (2007) in his study was also of the same view that an emotionally intelligent teacher promotes individual differences and develops his teaching strategy keeping in view those differences.

The result of the study also led us to the conclusion that teachers' EI skills and their demographic variables are interlinked with each other. Demographic variables including teachers' gender, marital status, and qualification are positively correlated. Only one facet under demographic variable i.e. age of the teacher was found irrelevant of EI skills.

The findings of the study concluded that female teachers display slightly better socio-emotional skills than their counterpart gender. They have better and healthy interpersonal skills with their students, teachers and administration. Some of the other studies also reported female workers as more socially handy as compared to their male co-workers (Mayer, Caruso and Salovey, 1999; Bransford et al., 2000, Lopes et al., 2006). Hayat et al., (2016), carried out a study to find out whether gender has any significant impact on EI of teachers and the result of the study revealed that female teachers at secondary schools were emotionally more intelligent and professionally mature than their male counterparts.

We can find the roots of these variations as a result of our socialization process and societal expectations from our female gender (Naghavi & Redzuan, 2011). This may be the result of our cultural influence that teaches women in a more socialized way not to express their anger, handle their problems with calmness, to be more affectionate and kind and adapt themselves according to demands of the situation. The study revealed very promising findings for female teachers as they do not lag in the teaching field as far as their EI is concerned. They can meet the changing demands of the profession more effectively as compare to their counterparts and can successfully handle difficulties faced during their job.

Findings of the present study found married teachers to some extent better than unmarried teachers in their EI skills. These findings are contrary to the findings of Landa et al., (2008) who found no significant difference in EI skills and marital status. Contrary to this, Birola et al., (2009), revealed that single teachers are more aware of their emotions, are more empathetic, and have improved social skills as compare to married teachers. The results of this study can be illuminated in terms of cultural differences. In Pakistani cultural context, both genders in Pakistan are taught throughout their life how to manage and be successful in their marital life, how to share their responsibilities and how to behave with others. They are taught to compromise with each other to make their relationship stronger. These responsibilities make them tolerant, patient, persistent and emotionally stable. These responsibilities demand better interpersonal skills, adaptability, flexibility, patience, stress tolerance, conflict management, awareness of one's duties and responsibilities and communication skills from marital partners. By possessing these traits they are considered as more emotionally intelligent than those who are unmarried. These traits also help married teachers control their emotions and adapt accordingly. Several other studies also reported EI of married individuals higher than those of single individuals (Vanishree, 2014; Ealias & George, 2012).

The result of the study found no significant difference in EI skills among different age groups of the study. An Australian study showed a weak significant relationship between age and EI (Palmer et al., 2002). While a big pile of researches exists supporting the fact that EI has a direct relationship with age (Bar On, et. al., 2000; Parker et al., 2005; Mayer, Salovey & Caruso, 2002). Dissimilarities and variations in findings may be due to very inclusive and diverse age groups in samples. For instance, BarOn (2004) viewed EI level of age groups ranging from 16-50+. He concluded that individuals in the lowest age group scored least on EI and all its sub factors and the next three groups are closely similar to each other. Sample in the present study varied from 23-50+ which shows that at this stage, individuals are grown up emotionally so they do not change positively afterward throughout their life. They are mature enough before they enter the teaching profession. They bring emotional stability to them. They also lack EI training in their professional lives. It is truly said that "age does not touch the stone of wisdom". If a person is not trained to be emotionally intelligent, EI cannot increase with the increase in age merely. In other words, it is just to say that EI is not as such affected by age as by formal training. While contemporary to our result, numerous studies exposed the higher level of EI with increasing age, and these findings made scholars believe that EI could elevate with age (BarOn, 1997).

The findings of the present study showed that qualification do affect EI positively. The qualification also guarantee enriched and enhanced socio-emotional intelligence. Saleh et al., (2019) study supported our claim that teachers with higher qualifications exhibit higher level of EI.

Findings of the study are in line with the results of several other studies that came up with similar results, (joseph & Brown, 2001) concluding that teachers with low EI skills were found to be less effective in their teaching profession. Ignat and Clipa (2012) inferred their results that teachers with emotional competencies and skills can cope with teaching challenges easily and effectively. But EI is the unrecognized segment of successful teaching (Mortiboys, 2005). According to Claxton (1999) encouraging the learning process does not include transference of information only, yet it involves managing mental nervousness and anxiety, and making rush or energy/thrill in the classroom. Some other studies also stated that to ensure our students are ready for life in the 21st century they need to be well equipped with a range of life and social skills such as being a creator, collaborator, communicator and critical thinker (4Cs) besides being capable of the 3Rs reading, writing and arithmetic. This can be achieved by allowing social and emotional development to occur and through linking socio-emotional abilities to everyday life during the learning process (Elias, 2012).

In developed countries, the concept of EI is now getting much more recognition and popularity. Organizations are focusing and emphasizing training sessions, seminars and conferences to improve EI of their employees. Goleman (1995) stated that the rules for work are shifting and one's capability can't only be evaluated and assessed by his/her ability to end up a task but by the ability to feel one self and others. Unluckily in our country, EI is still an unknown phenomenon and being neglected in sensitive professions like teaching. No efforts have been made to promote the EI of teachers by arranging any kind of seminar, workshop or conference.

Role of teacher is threefold; they do not only need to have an in-depth knowledge of the content they deliver but also requires them to be experts in various pedagogical and teaching methods to establish an inviting, challenging and supported learning environment (Mortiboys, 2012). The cornerstone supporting these two aspects however is the ability of the teacher to connect with their students, identifying emotional aspects of their learning journey and creating a safe and trusting environment through the use of EI. Before a teacher can understand a student's emotions and establish a deeper connection with them, they first need to have a high level of self-awareness as well as self-management of their own emotions and the impact those emotions can have on themselves and their students.

Several other studies are also in line with findings of this study as they stated that emotionally stable teacher can deliver knowledge in a proper, effective, and productive way, while those with low EI skills produce ineffective delivery of knowledge (Mehmood et al., 2013). EI is helpful for teachers in a way that it guides them to communicate clearly and effectively, can lead a group of people to create an environment inclusive for productive work, personal wellbeing, interactive at work as well as in their personal lives and make them successful in their profession (Hassan et al., 2015).

Many other researchers have established the same results showing a very positive relationship between teachers EI and TE (Fernandez Berocal & Ruiz, 2008; Drew, 2006; Hwang, 2007; Sutton & Wheatley, 2003; Wilson et al., 2009). An increasing number of researchers are also of the view that teachers' EI skills are of main importance for teacher effectiveness (McCown, Jensen, & Freedman, 2007; Sutton & Wheatley, 2003). It has also been claimed that teachers who are emotionally intelligent display more attention towards their students and can construct an emotionally healthy environment towards improved learning; while teachers with low EI skills are inefficient in the achievement of academic goals set for their students (Cotzee & Jensen, 2007; Ramana, 2013). Stein and Book (2000) found those teachers as the most effective who display high EI skills. Similarly, Haskett (2003) Hwang (2007) and Drew (2006) also found a significant relationship between various aspects of TE and EI skills.

We can conclude from the analysis and discussion of this study that teachers who realize and articulate themselves efficiently, understand students and their needs, who can maintain positive connotations and deal with daily stressors of the teaching profession, have better relations with their students, accurately manage classrooms, update their content knowledge, can widen the range of their pedagogical skills ultimately bear out to be effective teachers. The present study indicates that the emotionally intelligent behavior of a teacher results in his professional success and satisfaction. Emotional competencies of teachers are found to be of great contributing factor which has an impact on teaching-learning process as well as on the socio-emotional development of students in the classroom.

5.5   Recommendations

Although "the social and emotional competencies of the teachers have great impact on teaching-learning process" (Ergur, 2009, p. 1023) but teachers often miss the fundamental knowledge and skill of emotional and social growth in students and themselves.

The concept of emotional and social intelligence is a neglected area in Pakistan's education policies, so it must be given due space and consideration in education policies of the state.

The concept of EI is fairly a newly introduced term in under developing countries like Pakistan. So there is a need to organize a line of seminars, workshops, and conferences to create awareness among the masses about the significance of EI for success in personal and professional lives.

It has been found that during the recruitment phase socio-emotional skills of the teachers are completely ignored. So EI of teachers should be given due consideration in the recruitment and selection process.

Training programmes and courses should be designed and arranged to enhance socio-emotional skills or EI of already working professionals in teaching cadre, as it is a proven fact that EI can be taught at any stage of life.

In-service and pre-service teachers training programs should include courses related to EI.

EI development should become prominent and compulsory criteria in all the professional development programs of teachers.

Online EI refresher courses should be made a part of teachers' training programs to keep them updated with new emerging theories and practices of EI in the broad field of education.

The education system, and all the stake holders should come together on the same platform to create a comprehensive curriculum that will bring the concept of EI under the umbrella of the curriculum to enhance the EI of our upcoming generation for their wellbeing and success. The purpose of teaching should not only focus on the cognitive development of a child but it should focus on the social and emotional development of a child. Prominence and significance of EI be planned at schools, colleges, and university levels.

Curriculum developers should concentrate on the concept of EI skills into the class room setting to enhance the EI skills of students as well.

Principals of the schools should be trained to equip them with EI skills, so that they could be in a better position and have better skills to handle/tackle the psychological and social problems of their teachers that may affect their teaching-learning process.

Social media can play a crucial role in creating awareness among the masses about the effectiveness of EI skills and their impact on job performance.

5.6   Recommendations for Future Research

A Study can be conducted on how does the leadership style of a school principal affects EI and TE of teachers at school.

Further researches should be based on long-term or longitudinal effects of socio-emotional competencies of teachers on their students' academic performance. As students learning outcomes could be the best predictor of teacher's effectiveness.

An interview along with EI instruments can better elicit honest and authentic responses of teachers and students.

Class room observations will also be of crucial importance to evaluate teachers' EI skills and their TE.

Research studies may be conducted to explore the role of parents in enhancing EI skills among their children and their performance/behavior in Schools/colleges.

REFERENCES

Abraham, A. (2006). The need for integration of emotional intelligence skills in business education. *Business Renaissance Quarterly, 1*(3), 65-79

Abraham, R. (1999). Emotional Intelligence in organizations: A conceptualization. *Genetic, Social, and General Psychology Monographs, 2* (125), 209-224

Amritha, M., & Kadhiravan, M. (2006). Influence of Personality on the Emotional Intelligence of Teachers. *Edutracts, 5* (12), 25-29.

Anand, S.P. (1983). *Teacher Effectiveness in Schools. Journal of Indian Education, 8*(1), 3-12.

Anderson, L. (2004) *Increasing teacher effectiveness*, (2nd edition). UNESCO International Institute for Educational Planning. Retrieved on February 1, 2018, from http://unesdoc.unesco.org/images/0013/001376/137629e.pdf

Antoniou, A. S., Polychroni, F., & Kotroni, C. (2009). Working with Students with Special Educational Needs in Greece: Teachers' stressors and coping strategies. *International Journal of Special Education, 24,* 100-111

Aregbeyen, O. (2010). Students' perceptions of effective teaching and effective lecturer characteristics at the University of Ibadan, Nigeria. *Pakistan Journal of Social Sciences, 7* (2), 62-69.

Armstrong, T.S., Cohen, M.Z., Eriksen, L., & Cleeland, C. (2005). Content validity of self-report measurement instruments: an illustration from the development of the brain tumor module of the M.D. Anderson symptom inventory. *Oncol Nurs Forum, 32*(3), 669–76

Arnold, R. (2005). *Emphatic Intelligence: Teaching, learning and relating.* Sydney: UNSW Press.

Austin, E. J., Saklofske, D. H., & Egan, V. (2005). Personality, well-being and health correlates of trait emotional intelligence. *Personality and Individual Differences, 38*(3), 547-558.

Bachman, J., Stein, S., Campbell, K., & Sitarenios, G. (2000). Emotional intelligence in the collection of debt. *International Journal of Selection and Mafuzah Mohamad and Juraifa Jais / Procedia Economics and Finance, 35,* 674 – 682,

Baig, S. (2012). The personal values of school leaders in Pakistan: A contextual model of regulation and influence. *The Journal of Values-Based Leadership, 4* (2), 4.

Baker, J. P. & Berenbaum, H. (2007) Emotional approach and problem-focused coping: A comparison of potentially adaptive strategies. *Cognition and Emotion, 21*(1), 95-118.

Bar On, R. (1997). *Eq-I Baron Emotional Quotient Inventory Technical Manual.* Multi Health Systems Inc., Toronto.

Bar -On, R. (2004). In Glenn Geher (Ed.), *Measuring emotional intelligence: Common ground and controversy* (pp. 111-142). Hauppauge, NY: Nova Science Publishers.

Bar On, R., & Parker, J. (2000). *The handbook of emotional intelligence: Theory, development, assessment, and application at home, school, and in the workplace.* San Francisco, Jossey Bass, Inc.

Bar-On, R. (1997). *The Bar-On Emotional Quotient Inventory (EQ-I): A test of emotional intelligence.* Multi- Health Systems Inc., Toronto.

Bar-On, R. (2001). *Emotional Intelligence and Self Actualization, Emotional Intelligence in Everyday Life: A Scientific Inquiry.* New York, Psychology Press.

Bar-On, R. (2004). *The Bar-On Emotional Quotient Inventory (EQ-i): Rationale, description and summary of psychometric properties. Toronto,* Canada: Multi Health Systems.

Bar-On, R., & Handley, R. (2003a). *The Bar-On EQ-360.* Toronto, Canada: Multi Health Systems.

Bar-On, R., & Parker, J. (2011). *Emotional Intelligence Manual.* Bucharest: Old Court.

Basit, A., Rahman, F., Jumani, N. B., Chishti, S. H., & Malik, S. (2010). An analysis of conflict resolution strategies in Pakistani schools. *International Journal of Academic Research, 2*(6), 212-218.

Berliner, D.C. (1983). Developing Conceptions of Classroom Environment. *Educational Psychologist, 18,* 1-3.

Bhatti, R. (2009). Interpersonal relationships: students, teachers and librarians in University libraries of Pakistan. *Library Review, 58*(5), 362-371.

Bibi, F., Kazmi, S. F., Chaudhry, A. G., & Khan, S. E. (2015). Relationship between Emotional Intelligence and Coping Strategies among University Teachers of Khyber Pakhtunkhwa. *Pakistan Journal of Science, 67* (1), 81-84.

Birch, S. H., & Ladd, G. W. (1997). The teacher-child relationship and early school adjustment. *Journal of School Psychology, 55*(1), 61-79

Birola, C., Atamturka, H., & Fatou Silmana, F. (2009). Analysis of the emotional intelligence level of teachers. World Conference on Educational Sciences 2009. *Procedia Social and Behavioral Sciences, 1,* 2606–2614.

Bolton, D.L. (1969). The effect of various information formats on teacher selection decisions. *American Educational Research Journal, 6,* 329-347.

Boyatzis, R., Goleman, D., & Rhee, K. (2000). *Clustering competence in emotional intelligence: Insights for the emotional competence inventory.* In R. Bar-On and J. Parker, Handbook of Emotional Intelligence. San Francisco, Jossey-Bass Inc.

Boyd, J., Barnett, W. S., Bodrova, E., Leong, D. J., & Gomby, D. (2005). *Promoting children's social and emotional development through preschool (Preschool Policy Brief).* New Brunswick, NJ: National Institute for Early Education Research, Rutgers University.

Brackett, M. A., & Katulak, N. A. (2006). *Emotional intelligence in the classroom: Skill based training for teachers and students.* Applying emotional intelligence (pp.1-27). A practitioner's guide. New York, NY, US: Psychology Press.

Brackett, M. A., Rivers, S., Shiffman, S., Lerner, N., & Salovey, P. (2005). What is the best way to measure emotional intelligence? A case for performance measures. *Journal of Personality and Social Psychology Bulletin, 30,* 1018-1034.

Brackett, M.A., Rivers, S., & Salovey, P. (2005). *Emotional Intelligence and its relation to social, emotional, and academic outcomes among adolescents.* USA: Yale University.

Brackett, M.A., Rivers, S.E., & Salovey, P. (2011). Emotional intelligence: Implications for personal, social, academic, and workplace success. *Social and Personality Psychology Compass, 5*(1), 88–103.

Brophy, J. & Good, T. (1992). *Handbook of Research on Teaching*, (3rd Ed,), N.Y. Macmillan Publishing Company.

Brophy, J. (1983). Conceptualizing student motivation. *Educational Psychologist, 18*, 200-215.

Brotheridge, C., & Grandey, A. (2002). Emotional labor and burnout: Comparing two perspectives of people work. *Journal of Vocational Behavior, 60*, 17 - 39.

Butt, M. N. (2011). *Impact of non-verbal communication on students' learning outcomes.* Published PhD dissertation, Sarhad University of Science and Information Technology, Peshawar, Pakistan.

Campbell, A. & Ntobedzi, A. (2007). Emotional intelligence, coping and psychological distress: A partial least squares approach to developing a predictive model. *Electronic Journal of Applied Psychology: Emotional Intelligence, Coping and Psychological Distress, 3*(1), 39-54.

Carmeli, A., & Josman, Z. E. (2006). The relationship among emotional intelligence, task performance, and organizational citizenship behaviors. *Human Performance, 19*(4), 403-419.

Carson, C.C., Huelskamp, R.M., & Woodall, T.D. (1993). Perspectives on education in America. *Journal of Educational Research, 86*, 259- 311.

Chadha, N. K., & Singh, D. (2001). How to Measure your EQ, In Singh,D. E*motional Intelligence at Work: A Professional Guide*. New Delhi: Response Books

Chan, D. W. (2008). Emotional intelligence, self-efficacy, and coping among Chinese prospective and in-service teacher in Hong Kong. *Educational Psychology: An International Journal of Experimental Educational Psychology, 28*(4), 397-408.

Chan, D.W. (2004). Perceived emotional intelligence and self-efficacy among Chinese secondary school teachers in Hong Kong. *Personality and Individual Differences, 36*, 1781-1795

Chang, K.B. T. (2006). *Can we teach emotional intelligence?* Published PhD dissertation, University of Hawaii at Manoa. Retrieved from http://books.google.com/Books/about/Can_We_Teach_Emotional_Intelligene html? Retrieved on December 12, 2017

Chaudhry, A. A., & Usman, A. (2011). An investigation of the relationship between employees' emotional intelligence and performance. *African Journal of Business Management, 5*(9), 3556-3562.

Chechi, K. V. (2012). Emotional intelligence and teaching. *International Journal of Research in Economics & Social Sciences, 2* (2), 297–304.

Chughtai, A. A., & Zafar, S. (2006). Antecedents and consequences of organizational commitment among Pakistani university teachers. *Applied HRM Research, 11*(1), 39-64.

Claxton, G. (1999). *Wise up: The challenge of lifelong learning.* London: Bloomsbury.

Coetzee, M., & Jansen, C. (2007). *Emotional intelligence in the classroom: The secret of happy teachers.* South Africa: Juta.

Cohen, J. & Sandy S. (2007). The social, emotional and academic education of children: Theories, goals, methods and assessments. In R. Bar-On, J.G. Maree, & M.J. Elias   (Eds.), *Educating People to Be Emotionally Intelligent* (pp. 63-78).

Cooper, R. K., & Sawaf, A. (1997). *Executive EQ: Emotional intelligence in leadership and organizations.* New York: Grosset/Putnam.

Cotezee, M. & Jensen, C. (2007). *Emotional Intelligence in the Classroom: The Secret of Happy Teachers.* Cape Town: Juta & Co.

Darling-Hammond, L. (2000). Teacher quality and student achievement: A review of state policy evidence. *Educational Policy Analysis Archives, 8* (1).

Davis, J., & Wilson, S. (2000). Principals' efforts to empower teachers: Effects on teacher motivation and job satisfaction and stress. *The Clearing House, 73,* 349 353.

Delaney, J., Johnson, A.N., Johnson, T.D. &. Treslan, D.L (2010). *Students' perceptions of effective Teaching in higher education.* Memorial University of Newfoundland, Distance Education and Learning Technologies.

Di Fabio, A., & Palazzeschi, L. (2009). Emotional intelligence, personality traits and career decision difficulties. *International Journal for Educational and Vocational Guidance, 9* (2), 135-146.

Di Fabio,A., & Palazzeschi, L. (2008). Emotional intelligence and self-efficacy in a sample of Italian high school teachers. *Social Behavior and Personality, 6* (3), 315-326.

Donaldso-Feider, E. J., & Bond, F. W. (2004). The relative importance of psychological acceptance and emotional intelligence to workplace wellbeing. *British Journal of Guidance & Counseling, 32,* 187-204.

Doyle, A. (2012). *Emotional intelligence: Emotional Intelligence Test.* The New York Company. Retrieved from http://jobsearch.about.com/od/personalitytests/g/ emotional intelligence.htm on June 15, 2018.

Drew, T. (2006). *The relationship between emotional intelligence and student teacher performance.* Published PhD dissertation, University of Nebraska.

Ealias, A., & George, J. (2012). Emotional intelligence and job satisfaction: A Correlational study. Research. *Journal of Commerce & Behavioral Science, 1*(4), 37-42.

Edward, D. B. (1973). *Lateral thinking: Creativity Step by Step.* New York, Perennial Library.

Elementary and Secondary Education Department Khyber Pakhtunkhwa- official web portal. (n.d.). Elementary and Secondary Education Department Khyber Pakhtunkhwa-official web portal. Retrieved March 2015, from http://kpese.gov.pk/

EMIS (Educational Management Information System). (2015). *Annual Statistical Report of Schools: Peshawar.* Government of Khyber Pakhtunkhwa, Pakistan.

Ergur, Derya. (2009). How can education professionals become emotionally intelligent?. Procedia-Social and Behavioral Sciences. 1. 1023-1028. 10.1016/j.sbspro.2009.01.183.

Fariselli, L., Ghini, M. & Freedman, J. (2008). Age and emotional intelligence. White Paper. Retrieved from: http://www.6seconds.org/sei/media /WP_EQ_and_Age.pdf on August 22, 2018.

Fatt, J. P., & Howe, C. K. (2003). Emotional intelligence of foreign and local university students in Singapore: Implications for managers. *Journal of Business and Psychology, 17*(3), 345-367.

Feldman, D.H. (1999). *The Development of Creativity: Handbook of Creativity.* Cambridge University Press.

Feldman, K. A. (1988). Effective college teaching from the students' and faculty's view: Matched or mismatched priorities? *Research in Higher Education, 28* (4), 291 344.

Fer, S. (2004). Qualitative Evaluation of Emotional Intelligence In-Service Program for Secondary School Teachers. *The Qualitative Report, 9*(4), 562-588. Retrieved from https://nsuworks.nova.edu/tqr/vol9/iss4/1

Fernandez-Berrocal,P & Ruiz,D. (2008). Emotional Intelligence in Education. *Journal of Research in Educational Psychology, 6* (2), 421-436.

Fernandez-Berrocal,P., & Ramos, N., P. (2008). Extrema. Perceived Emotional Intelligence Facilitates Cognitive Emotional processes of adaptation to an acute stressor. *Cognition and Emotion, 21*(4), 758-772

Flander, N.A. & Simon, R. (1969). *Teacher Effectiveness in Robert Eels: Encyclopedia of Educational Research,* (4th ed., pp. 142-143). London: Mc. Million.

Fullen, M., & Hargreaves, A. (1992). *Teacher Development and Educational Change.* The Falmer Press.

Gardner, H. (1983). Frames of mind: The theory of multiple intelligences. New York, NY: Basic books. Fontana Press.

Gay, L. R., Mills, G. E., & Airasian, P. W. (2012). Educational research: Competencies for analysis and applications. Boston: Pearson.

George, J. M. (2000). Emotions and leadership: The role of emotional intelligence. *Human relations, 53* (8), 1027-1055.

Ghanizadeh, A. & Moafian, F. (2010). The role of EFL teachers' emotional intelligence in their success. *ELT Journal, 64*(4), 424-435.

Ghanizadeh, A., & Moafian. (2010). The role of EFL teachers' emotional intelligence in their success. *ELT Journal, 64* (4), 424-435.

Goad, D. (2005). *Emotional intelligence and teacher retention.* Institute of emotional intelligence, Texas, A& M University Kingsville, Kingsville, TX.

Goleman, D. (1995). *Emotional Intelligence.* New York, NY: Bantam Books.

Goleman, D. (1998). *Working with Emotional Intelligence.* New York, Bantam.

Goleman, D. (1998). IQ and technical skills are important, but emotional intelligence is the sine qua non of leadership. *Harvard Business Review, 93*(1), 93-102.

Goleman, D. (1998). *Working with emotional intelligence* (p-12). New York: Bantam.

Goleman, D. (2001). *An emotional intelligence based theory of performance in the emotionally intelligent workplace.* New York, NY: Jossey-Bass.

Goleman, D. (2001). An EI-based theory of Performance. In Cherniss and D. Goleman, (Eds.). *The emotionally intelligent workplace.* John Wiley & Sons, Inc. Retrieved from http: //www.careacademy. org/elmp/ Documents / Goleman % 20 EI% 20 % 20 Issues % 20 in % 20 Paradigm % 20 Building.pdf

Goleman, D. (2004). *Emotional Intelligence: working with emotional intelligence.* London: Bloomsbury Publishing.

Goleman, D. (2006) Social Intelligence: *The new science of social relationships.* New York, NY: Bantam Books.

Goleman, D., & Cherniss, C. (2001). *The emotionally intelligent workplace: How to select for, measure, and improve emotional intelligence in individuals, groups, and organizations.* Jossey-Bass.

GU, Q., & Day, C. (2007). Teacher's resilience: A necessary condition for effectiveness. *Teaching and Teacher Education, 23*(8), 1302-1316.

Gupta, J., & Kaur, R. (2006). Emotional Intelligence among prospective teachers. *Journal of community Guidance and Research, 23*(2), 133-140.

Hakanen, J. J., Bakker, A. B., & Schaufeli, W. B. (2006). Burnout and work engagement among teachers. *Journal of School Psychology, 43*, 495–513.

Hanif, R. (2004). *Teacher stress, job performance and self-efficacy of women school teachers.* Published PhD thesis. Quaid-e-Azam University, Islamabad, Pakistan.

Haq, M.A., Anwar, S., & Hassan, M. (2017). Impact of emotional intelligence on teacher's performance in higher education institutions of Pakistan. *Future Business Journal,* 3(2), 87-97. Retrieved from https://www.sciencedirect.com

Hargreaves, A. (1998). The emotional practice of teaching. *Teaching and teacher education, 14*(8), 835-854.

Hargreaves, A. (2000). Mixed emotions: Teachers' perceptions of their interactions with students. *Teaching and teacher education, 16*(8), 811-826.

Hargreaves, A., & Fullen, M. (1998). *Teacher Development and Educational Change.* The Falmer Press.

Haskett, R. (2003). Emotional intelligence and teaching success in higher education. Doctoral dissertation. Indiana University.

Haskett, R. A., & Bean, J. P. (2003). *Emotional intelligence and Teaching Success In higher education.* UMI.

Hassan, F., Chew, B. & Zain, A.M. (2015). The relationship between the social management of emotional intelligence and academic performance among medical students. *Psychology, Health & Medicine, 20(*2), 198-204.

Hassan, N., Hayati, M.D., Jani, S., Som, R.M., Hamid, N, Z.A., & Azizam, N.A. (2015). The Relationship between Emotional Intelligence and Teaching Effectiveness among Lecturers at Universiti Teknologi MARA, Puncak Alam, Malaysia. *International Journal of Social Science and Humanity, 5*(1), 1-5.Retrieved on November 2, 2018 from

http://www.ijssh.org/papers/411H00001.pdf.

Hawkey, K. (2006). Emotional intelligence and mentoring in pre-service teacher education: A literature review. *Mentoring & Tutoring, 14*(2), 137-147.

Hayat, I., Bibi, T., and Ambreen, M. (2016). Gender influence on emotional intelligence and professional development among secondary school teachers. *Science International (Lahore), 28*(1), 645-652.

Hess, J., & Bacigalupo, A. (2010). Emotionally intelligent leader, the dynamics of knowledge based organizations and the role of emotional intelligence in organizational development. *On the Horizon, 18,* (3), 222-229.

Hwang, F. F. (2007). *The relationship between emotional intelligence and teaching effectiveness.* Dissertation Texas and M University – Kingsville, United States.

Ignat, A.A., & Clipa, O. (2012). Teachers' satisfaction with life, job satisfaction and their emotional intelligence. *Procedia-Social and Behavioral Sciences, 33,* 498-502.

Isen, A.M. (1993). *Positive affect and decision making.* In Handbook of emotions, ed. M Lewis and J. Havilland, (pp. 261- 277). New York: Guilford Press.

Ismail, N., & Idris, K. N. (2009). The effects of classroom communication on students: academic performance at the International Islamic University Malaysia (IIUM). *Unitar e-journal, 5*(1), 37.

Iurea, C., Neacsu, I., Safta, C. G., & Suditu, M. (2011). The study of the relation between the teaching methods and the learning styles: The impact upon the students' academic conduct.*Procedia Social and Behavioral Sciences, 11,* 256-260.

Jadhav, V., & Patil, A. K. (2010). Emotional Intelligence among student teachers in relation to general Intelligence and academic achievement. *Edutrack, 10* (3), .36-37.

Jahangiri, L., Mucciolo, T. W., Choi, M., & Spielman, A. I. (2008). Assessment of teaching effectiveness in US dental schools and the value of triangulation. *Journal of dental education, 72*(6), 707-718.

Jennings, P. A., & Greenberg, M. T. (2009). The prosaically classroom: Teacher social and emotional competence in relation to student and classroom. *Review of Educational Research, 79,* (1) 491-525

Jerome, K. L. (2010). An Examination of the relationship between emotional intelligence and the leadership styles of early childhood professionals. *Dissertation International, 70* (09), 3336A.

Jhaa, A., & Singh, I. (2012). Teacher Effectiveness in Relation to Emotional Intelligence among Medical and Engineering Faculty Members. *Europe's Journal of Psychology, 8*(4), 667685

Joseph, J., & Brown, K. (2001). *Starting out: The beginning teacher's companion.* London: Focus Education

Jossey- Lyubomirsky, S., King, L., & Diener, E. (2005). The Benefits of frequent positive affect: does happiness lead to success? *Psychological Bulletin, 131*(6), 803-855.

Justice, M. (2005). *Emotional intelligence and teacher education and practice. Institute of emotional intelligence.* Texas, A& M University Kingsville, Kingsville, TX.

Katyal, S., & Awasthi, E. (2017). Gender differences in emotional intelligence among adolescents of Chandigarh. *Journal of Human Ecology, 17*(2), 153- 155.

Kaur, M., & Talwar, A. (2014). Teaching Competency of Secondary School Teachers In Relation To Emotional Intelligence. *International Journal of Learning, Teaching and Educational Research, 3* (1) 83-90.

Kauts, D.S. (2016). Emotional Intelligence and Academic Stress among College Students. *Educational Quest: An Int. J. of Education and Applied Social Sciences, 7* (3).

Keefer, K. V., Parker, J.D., & Wood, L. (2012). Trait emotional intelligence and university graduation outcomes using latent profile analysis to identify students at risk for degree no completion. *Journal of Psycho-educational Assessment, 30*(4), 402-413.

Khan, R. A. & Kamal, A. (2010). *Self-report measure of emotional intelligence scale.* Centre of Excellence, National Institute of Psychology, Quaid-e-Azam University, Islamabad, Pakistan.

Khani, M. (2010). *Investigation of the relationship between the manager's transformational and pragmatic leadership styles and emotional intelligence in bank branch mashhad.* Ferdowsi University of Mashhad, Faculty of Social Science, Iran.

Kim, C.Y. (2002). Teachers in Digital Knowledge-Based Society: New Roles and Vision. *Asia Pacific Education Review, 3* (2), 144-148.

Krejcie, R.V., & Morgan, D.W., (1970). *Determining Sample Size for Research Activities.* Educational and Psychological Measurement.

Kremenitzer, J. P., & Miller, R. (2008). Are you a highly qualified, emotionally intelligent early childhood educator?. *Young Children, 63*, 106–112.

Kunter, M., Vieluf, S., & Van De Vijver, F. J. R. (2013). Teacher self-efficacy in cross national perspective. *Teaching and Teacher Education, 35*, 92–103

Labaree, D. F. (2000). On the Nature of Teaching and Teacher Education Difficult Practices That Look Easy. *Journal of Teacher Education, 51*(3), 228-233.

Landa, J. A., Lopez-Zafra, E., Martos, M. P. B., & Aguilar-Luzon M. C. (2008). The relationship between emotional intelligence, occupational stress and health in nurses: A questionnaire survey. *International Journal of Nursing Studies, 45*, 888-90.

Latif, H., Majoka, M.I., & Khan, M.I. (2018). Emotional intelligence and job performance of high school female teachers. Pakistan journal of psychological research, 33(2).

Leedy, G. M., & Smith, J. E. (2012) Development of emotional intelligence of first year undergraduate students in a frontier state. *College Student Journal, 46*(4), 795-804.

Lenka, S.K. & Kant, R. (2012). Emotional intelligence of secondary school teachers in relation to their professional development. *Asian Journal of Management Sciences and Education, 1*(1), 90.

Lewis, R. (1999). Teachers coping with the stress of classroom discipline. *Social Psychology of Education, 3*, 155-171.

Lopes, P. N., Grewal, D., Kadis, J., Gall, M. & Salovey, P. (2006). Evidence that emotional intelligence is related to job performance and affect and attitudes at work. *Psicothema, 18*, 132-138.

Lopes, P. N., Salovey, P., Cote, S., & Beers, M. (2005). Emotion regulation abilities and the quality of social interaction. *Emotion, 5*, 113–118.

Lopez, S.J. (2007). *Positive Psychology*. Sage Publications, New Delhi, India

Low, G.R., & Nelson, D.A. (2004). *Emotional Intelligence: Effectively bridging the gap between high school and college*. Texas Study Magazine for Secondary Education, Spring Edition

Lunerbrug. F.C. (1996). *Educational Administration*. Wards Worth Publishing Co.

Mahmood, Z., Habib,S., & Saleem,S. (2013). Development and Validation of Social Intelligence Scale for University Students. *National Institute of Psychology, 28*(1).

Mahmud, A. (2013). *Emotional intelligence on the performance of university teachers at Punjab University*. Published Ph.D Dissertation. Institute of Education and Research, University of the Punjab, Lahore.

Malik, M. E., Nawab, S., Naeem, B., & Danish, R. Q. (2010). Job satisfaction and organizational commitment of university teachers in public sector of Pakistan. *International Journal of Business and Management, 5*(6), 17-26.

Malik, S.Z., & Sehrish, S. (2016). Effect of Emotional Intelligence on Academic Performance among Business Students in Pakistan. *Bulletin of Education and Research, 38*(1), 197-   208

Mayer, J. D. & Salovey, P. (1997). *What is Emotional Intelligence? Emotional Development and Emotional Intelligence:* Implications for Educators, (p-10). New York, NY: Basic Books.

Mayer, J. D. (2001). *A Field Guide to Emotional Intelligence, Emotional Intelligence and Everyday life.* New York, NY: Psychology Press.

Mayer, J. D., & Salovey, P. (1997). What is emotional intelligence: In Salovey, & D. Slutyer (Eds.)? *Emotional development and emotional intelligence: Implications for educators,* (pp. 3-31). New York: Basic Books.

Mayer, J. D., Caruso, D. R., & Salovey, P. (1999). Emotional intelligence meets traditional standards for an intelligence. Intelligence, 27, 267–298.

Mayer, J. D., Salovey, & P., Caruso, D.R. (2000). Models of emotional intelligence. In Sternberg (Ed.), *Handbook of intelligence.* Cambridge, UK: Cambridge University Press.

Mayer, J. D., Salovey, P., & Caruso, D. (2002). *The Mayer-Salovey-Caruso Emotional Intelligence Test (MSCEIT),* (Version 2.0). Toronto, Canada: Multi-Health Systems.

Mayer, J. D., Salovey, P., & Caruso, D. R. (2002).Mayer–Salovey–Caruso Emotional Intelligence Test (MSCEIT) user's manual. Toronto, ON: MHS Publishers.

Mayer, J.D., & Patrick J.S. (2008). Investigating aspects of self-criticism and emotional intelligence in university students. *Dissertation Abstract International, 68* (10), 4200-A.

McBer, H. (2000). *Research into teacher effectiveness: a model of teacher effectiveness.* Retrieved from http:// ateneu.xtec.cat on December 2, 2017.

McCarthy, C. J., Lineback, S., & Reiser, J. (2015). Teacher stress, emotion, and classroom management. In E. T. Emmer & E. J. Sabornie (Eds.), *Handbook of classroom management* (2nd ed., 301–321). New York: Routledge.

McClelland, D. C. (1973). Testing for competence rather than intelligence. *American Psychologist, 28* (1), 1.

McCown, K., Jensen, A.L. & Freedman J. (2007). The Self-Science approach to social emotional learning. In R. Bar-On, J.G. Maree and M.J. Elias (Eds.), *Educating People to Be Emotionally Intelligent* (pp. 109-122). Westport, CT: Praeger.

McLean, L., & Connor, C. M. (2015). Depressive symptoms in third grade teachers: Relations to classroom quality and student achievement. *Child Development, 86,* 945-954

Medley, D.M. & Coker, H. (1987). The accuracy of principals' judgments of teacher performance. *Journal of Educational Research, 80* (4), 242-247.

Mehmood, T., Qasim, S., & Azam, R. (2013). Impact of Emotional Intelligence on the Performance of University Teachers. International Journal of Humanities and Social Science, 3(18), 300.

Mendes, E.J. (2003). *The relationship between emotional intelligence and occupational but out in secondary school teachers.* Dissertation Abstracts, 95008-284.

Mesquita, B., & Frijda, N. H. (1992). Cultural variations in emotions: A Review. *Psychological Bulletin,* 112, 179–204.

Mesquita, B., Frijda, N. H., & Scherer, R. K. (1997). Culture and emotion. In Handbook of cross cultural psychology, (Vol- 2). *Basic processes and human development*, ed. Berry, P.R. Dasen, and T.S. Saraswathi, 255 - 97. Boston: Allyn and Bacon.

Miller, A. L. (2010). *Cognitive processes associated with creativity: Scale development and validation. Dissertation Abstract International, 70* (11), 4179A.

Ming, L. F. (2003). Conflict management styles and emotional intelligence of faculty and staff at a selected college in southern Taiwan (China).Retrieved from www.eiconsortium.org on December 29, 2018.

Ministry of Education, P. 2009. National Education Policy 2009. Islamabad: Government of Pakistan.

Modupe, H.E. (2010). Emotional intelligence and self – esteem as predictors for success in teaching practice exercise. *Academic Leadership, 8,* (3).

Mohamad, M. & Jais, J. (2016). Emotional Intelligence and Job Performance: A Study among Malaysian Teachers. *7th International Economics & Business Management Conference, Procedia Economics and Finance, 35,* 674 – 682

Moon, T. (2010). A study on emotional intelligence correlates of the four-factor model of cultural Intelligence. *Journal of Managerial Psychology, 25* (8) 876-898.

Mortiboys, A. (2005). *Teaching with Emotional Intelligence.* London: Routledge.

Mortiboys, A. (2013). *Teaching with emotional intelligence: A step-by-step guide for higher and further education professionals. London:* Routledge.

Mucciolo, T. W., Jahangiri, L., Choi, M., & Spielman, A. I. (2008). Assessment of teaching effectiveness in US dental schools and the value of triangulation. *Journal of dental education, 72*(6), 707-718.

Mushtaq, N., Shakoor, A., Azeem, M., & Zia, N. (2012). Self-Esteem's difference among primary, elementary, secondary and higher secondary schools teachers. *International Journal of Humanities and Social Science, 2*(1), 200-205.

Naghavi, F., & Redzuan, M. (2011). The relationship between gender and emotional intelligence. *World Applied Sciences Journal, 15*(4), 555-561

Najmuddin, S. H. S., Noriah, M. I., & Mohamad, B. (2011). Impacts of emotional intelligence on work values of high school teachers. *Social and Behavioral Sciences, 30*, 1688- 1692.

Naqvi, I., H., Iqbal, M., Akhtar, S.N. (2016). the Relationship between Emotional Intelligence and Performance of Secondary School Teachers. Bulletin of Education and Research, 38 (1), 209-224

National Council of Teacher Education. (1998).*National Council of Teacher Education*. Government of Pakistan.

Neale, S., Spencer-Arnell, L., & Wilson, L. (2011). *Emotional intelligence coaching: improving performance for leaders, coaches and the individual.* Kogan Page. Relationship between Emotional Intelligence and Performance of SST- 224.

Nelis, D., Quoidbach, J., Mikolajczak, M., &Hansenne, M. (2009). Increasing emotional intelligence: How is it possible? *Personality and Individual Differences, 47*(1), 36-41.

Nelson, D.B.; Low, G.R.; Nelson, K. (2005). The Emotionally Intelligent Teacher: A Transformative Learning Model. Retrieved from http://www.tamuk.edu/ edu/kwei000/research/articles/article_files/emotionally_intelligent teacher.pdf

Oliver, R. M., & Reschly, D. J. (2010). Teacher preparation in classroom management: Implications for students with emotional and behavioral disorders. *Behavioral Disorders, 35*, 188-199

Oliver, R., Wehby, J., Daniel, J. (2011). Teacher classroom management practices: Effects on disruptive or aggressive student behavior. *Campbell Systematic Reviews, 4.*

Olson, D. H., McCubbin, H. I., Barnes, H. L., Muxen, M. J., Larsen, A. S., & Wilson, M.A (1989). *Families: What makes them work?* California: Sage Publications.

Palmer, B., Donaldson, C., & Stough. (2002). Emotional intelligence and life satisfaction. *Personality and Individual Differences, 33*, 1091–1100.

Palmer, P.J. (1997). *The Courage to Teach.* San Francisco: Jossey Bass

Palomera, R., Fernandez-Berrocal, F., Brackett, M. (2008). Emotional intelligence as a basic competency in pre-service teacher training: some evidence. *Electronic Journal of Research in Educational Psychology, 16* (2), 437- 454.

Parker, J. D., Creque, R. E., Barnhart, D. L., Harris, J. I., Majeski, S. A., Wood, L.M., & Hogan, M. J. (2004). Academic achievement in high school: does emotional intelligence matter? *Personality and Individual Differences, 37*(7), 1321-1330.

Parker, J. D., Hogan, M. J., Eastabrook, J.M., Oke, A., & Wood, L. M (2005).\ Emotional intelligence and student retention: Predicting the successful transition from high school to university. *Personality and Individual Differences, 41*(7), 1329-1336. Retrieved from http://www.sciencedirect.com

Parker, J.D., Creques, R., Harris, J., Majeski, S.A., Wood, L.M., Hogan. M.J (2003). Academic Success in High School: Does Emotional Matter? *ERIC Clearing House.*

Pathan, Y., G. et al. (2004). Emotional Intelligence of Secondary teachers at D.Ed. Collegeat Navaput, Maharashtra. *Edutracts, 6* (1), 37-38.

Payne, W. L. (1985). A study of emotion: developing emotional intelligence; self-integration; relating to fear, pain and desire. *The union for experimenting colleges and universities, 47,*(01a), 0203. Retrieved from http://eqi.org/payne.htm

Penrose, A., Perry, C., & Ball, I. (2007). Emotional intelligence and teacher self-efficacy: The contribution of teacher status and length of experience. *Educational Research, 17*(1), 107-126.

Pianta, R.C. (2006). Classroom management and relationships between children and teachers: Implications for research and practice. In C.M Everston and C.S. Weinstein (Eds.), Handbook of *Classroom Management: Research, Practice and Contemporary Issues* (pp. 685-710).

Powell, W., & Kusuma-Powell, O. (2010). *Becoming an emotionally intelligent teacher.* Corwin Press.

Prati, L. M., Douglas, C., Ferris, G. R., Ammeter, A. P., Buckley, M. R. (2003). Emotional intelligence, leadership effectiveness, and team outcomes. *International Journal of Organizational Analysis, 11,* 21–4

Qualter, P. Whiteley, H., Morley, A. & Dudiak, H. (2009). The role of emotional intelligence in the decision to persist with academic studies in HE. *Research in Post-Compulsory Education, 14*(3), 219-231. Retrieved from http://www.heacademy.ac.

Raider-Roth, M. (2005). *Trusting What You Know: The High Stakes of Classroom Relationships.* Indianapolis, IN: Jossey-Bass.

Ramana T.V. (2003). *Interstate Analysis of Different Dimensions of Educational growth India.* Published thesis. Andhra University Visakhapatnam.

Ramana, T.V. (2013). Emotional Intelligence and Teacher Effectiveness -An Analysis. V*oice of Research, 2*(2).

Rani, K.V. & Porgio, G. (2010). *Academic achievements of higher secondary student relation to their multiple intelligence, critical thinking and creativity.* Published doctoral dissertation, M.S. University, Tirunelveli.

Robert, E. (1996). *Creativity games for trainers: a handbook of group activities for jumpstarting workplace creativity.* New York, NY: Training McGraw-Hill.

Rohana, N., Kamaruzaman, J., & Zanariah, A. R. (2009). Emotional intelligence of Malaysian academia towards work performance. *International Education Studies, 2*, 103-112.

Rubin L. (1984). *Artistry in Teaching.* New York: Random House.

Rubio, D, M. Berg-Wegwe, M., Tebb, S.S., Lee, E.S., & Rauch, S. (2003). Objectifying content validity: conducting a content validity study in social work. *Social work research, 7*, 96.

Salami, O. S. (2007). Relationships of Self-efficacy and Emotional Intelligence with Work Attitudes among Secondary School Teachers in Southwestern Nigeria. *Pakistan Journal of Social Sciences, 4*(4), 540-547.

Salami, S. O. (2010). Occupational stress and well-being: Emotional intelligence, self-efficacy, coping, negative affectivity and social support as moderators. *The Journal of International Social Research, 3*(12), 387-398.

Salovey, P., & Mayer, J. D. (1990). Emotional intelligence. *Imagination, cognition and personality, 9*(3), 185-211.

Salovey, P., Mayer, J.D., & Caruso, D. (1995). *The positive psychology of emotional intelligence: The handbook of positive psychology.* New York: Oxford University Press.

Schutte, N., Malouff J., & Hine, D. (2011). The association of ability and trait emotional intelligence with alcohol problems. *Addiction Theory and Research, 19* (3), 260-265.

Schutte, N.S., Malouff, J.M., Bhullar, N. (2009). The assessing emotions scale. In C. Stough, D.H. Saklofske, & J. D.A. Parker (Ed) *assessing emotional intelligence: Theory, research, and applications* (pp.119–134). New York, NY: Springer.

Shafiq, M., & Rana, A. R. (2016). Relationship of emotional intelligence to organizational commitment of college teachers in Pakistan. *Eurasian Journal of Educational Research, 62,* 1-1

Shah, M. (2011). *Teacher collegiality and commitment in high-and low-achieving secondary schools in Islamabad.* Published PhD dissertation, Pakistan. Retrieved from https://www.grin.com on November 11, 20117.

Shah. M. (2006). Emotional intelligence of upper primary students of Gujarat state in relation to certain variables. Unpublished Ph.D dissertation, Sardar Patel University. Vidyanagar, Gujarat.

Shahzad, S. (2012). *Relationship between teachers' emotional intelligence and their teaching effectiveness.* Published PhD dissertation. Institute of education and research, university of the Punjab, Lahore.

Shehzad. S., & Mahmood, N. (2013). Gender Differences in Emotional Intelligence of University Teachers. *Pakistan Journal of Social and Clinical Psychology, 11* (1), 16-21

Sieberer-Nagle, K. (2016).Effective Classroom-Management & Positive Teaching English Language Teaching. *Canadian Center of Science and Education, 9* (1)163.

Singh, D. (2003). *Emotional Intelligence at work: A professional guide.* New Delhi: Sage.

Singh, J.D., (2015). A study of emotional intelligence of teacher educators In relation to certain demographical variables. *Scholarly research journal for interdisciplinary studies, 3*(17), 2883-2893.

Singh, P. (2008). A study of achievements among general and scheduled caste students in relation to emotional intelligence. *Journal of educational studies, 6*(2), pp.49-52.

Siraj ud Din, K, B., Rehman, R., & Bibi, Z. (2011). An investigation of conflict management in public and private sector universities. *African Journal of Business Management, 5*(16), 6981-6990.

Smith, N. (2008). *Measurement of emotional intelligence in African-American adolescents: Testing the validity and reliability of an original instrument.* Dissertation Abstract International, 68 (12), 4990A.

Song, L., Huang, G., Peng, K., Law, K., Wong, C., & Chen, Z. (2010). The differential effect of general mental ability and emotional intelligence on academic performance and   social interactions. *Intelligence, 38*(1), 137-143.

SRMEI. (2010). *Self-report Measure of Emotional Intelligence* (2010). Technical Manual. Islamabad Pakistan: National Institute of Psychology.

Stein S.J. & Book, H.E. (2000). *The EQ Edge – Emotional Intelligence and Your Success.* Toronto: MHS.

Stein, S., Book, H., & Kanoy, K. (2013). *The student EQ edge: Emotional intelligence and your academic and personal success.* San Francisco, CA: Jossey-Bass.

Sternberg, R. J. (1999). *Handbook of Creativity.* New York: Cambridge   University Press.

Sutton, R. E. (2004). Emotional regulation goals and strategies of teachers. *Social Psychology of Education, 7,*379-398

Sutton, R. E., & Wheatley, K. F. (2003). Teachers' emotions and teaching: A review of the literature and directions for future research. *Educational psychology review, 15*(4), 327-358.

Tabassum, F., & Ali, M. A. (2012). Professional self-esteem of secondary school teachers. *Asian Social Science, 8*(2), 206.

Tajudin, A.F.A., Omar, C.M.Z.C., Yunus, N.K.Y., Aziz, R.A., & Had, N.F.A. (2014). The Effect of Emotional Intelligence and Job Stress on the Teaching

Effectiveness among Malaysia Polytechnic Lecturers. *International Journal of Sciences: Basic and Applied Research (IJSBAR) 17*(1), 226-23. Retrieved from http://gssrr.org/index.php

Thomas, M. (2008). *Effective Teaching*. New Delhi: S. Chand & Company Ltd, India.

Thorndike, E. L. (1920). Intelligence and its uses. *Harper's Magazine, 140,* 227-235. Retrieved from https://harpers.org/archive/1920/01/intelligence-and-its-uses/, on January 1, 2018.

Thorndike, R. L., & Stein, S. (1937). An evaluation of the attempts to measure social intelligence. *Psychological Bulletin, 34*(5), 275.

Titsworth, S., Quinlan, M., & Mazer, J. (2010). Emotion in teaching and learning: Development and validation of the classroom emotions scale. *Communication Education, 59* (4), 431- 452.

Todd, L. (2006). *The Relationship between Emotional Intelligence and Student Teacher Performance*.Ph.D. dissertation published, University of Nebraska, 2006.

Topno, I. (2011). *Emotional Intelligence, Creativity and Teacher Effectiveness Of Primary School Teachers*. Ph.D published dissertation. Department of Education, Manonmaniam Sundaranar University, Tmilnadu, India. Retrieved from http://hdl.handle.net/10603/23996 on November 28, 2018.

Walsh, D., & Maffei, M. J. (1994). Never in a class by themselves: An examination of behaviors affecting the student-professor relationship. *Journal on Excellence in College Teaching, 5*(2), 23-49.

Warr, P., Cook, J., & Wall, T. (1979). Scales for the measurement of some work attitudes and   aspects of psychological well-being. *Journal of Occupational Psychology, 52,* 129- 148

Wechsler, D. (1949). *Manual for the Wechsler intelligence Scale for children.* New York: The Psychological Corporation.

Weisinger, H. (1998). *Emotional intelligence at work.* San Francisco: Jossey-Bass.

Williams, M., & Burden, R. (2000). *Psychology of Language Teachers: A Social Constructivist Approach.* Cambridge: Cambridge University Press

Wilson, b & Corbett, d. (2002). What urban students say about good teaching? *Educational leadership, 60, 18-22.*

Wilson, E., Demetriou, H., & Winterbottom, M. (2009). The role of emotion in teaching: are there differences between male and female newly qualified teachers' approaches to teaching? *Educational Studies, 35*(4), 449–473.

Wols, A., Scholte, R.H.J., & Qualter, P. (2015). Prospective associations between loneliness and emotional intelligence. Journal of Adolescence, 39, 40 48.

Wong, C., & Law, K.S. (2002). The effects of leader and follower emotional intelligence on performance and attitude: An exploratory study. *Leadership Quarterly, 13* (3), 243-274.

Wong, C., Wong, C., Peng, K. et al., (2010). Effect of middle-level leader and teacher emotional intelligence on school teachers' job satisfaction. *Educational Management   Administration & Leadership, 38* (1), 59-70.

Wood, R., & Tolley, H. (2003). Inteligenţa emoţională prin teste. Cum să vă evaluaţi şi să văcreşteţi inteligenţa emoţională. Bucureşti (*Emotional intelligence through tests. How to evaluate and increase your emotional intelligence.* Bucharest): Meteor Press.

Woolfork, A., Hughes, M., & Walkup, V. (2008). *Psychology in Education.* New York: Pearson Longman.

Zamanzadeh, V., Ghahramanian, A., Rassouli, M., Abbaszadeh, A., & Alavi, H.(2015). Design and implementation content validity Study: development of an instrument for measuring patient-centered communication. *Journal of Caring Science, 4* (5), 165–78.

Zeidner, M., Matthews, G., & Roberts, R. D. (2001). Slow Down, You Move Too Fast: emotional Intelligence Remains an "Elusive" Intelligence. *Emotion, 1*(3), 265-275.